STIRLING LEGENDS

Edited by Zillah J. Jamieson

Stirling Legends edited by Zillah J. Jamieson for Stirling District Tourism.

First edition published in Great Britain in 2022 by Extremis Publishing Ltd., Suite 218, Castle House, 1 Baker Street, Stirling, FK8 1AL, United Kingdom.
www.extremispublishing.com

Extremis Publishing is a Private Limited Company registered in Scotland (SC509983) whose Registered Office is Suite 218, Castle House, 1 Baker Street, Stirling, FK8 1AL, United Kingdom.

Copyright © Zillah J. Jamieson and Stirling District Tourism, 2022.

The contributors to this collection have asserted the moral right under the Copyright, Designs and Patents Act 1988 to be identified as the authors of this work.

Stirling District Tourism Ltd. and the Stirling District Tourism logo are Copyright © Stirling District Tourism Ltd., which is a Private Limited Company registered in Scotland (SC156924) and a Registered Scottish Charity (SC023597).

The views expressed in this work are solely those of the authors, and do not necessarily reflect those of the publisher. The publisher hereby disclaims any responsibility for them.

This book is a work of non-fiction. Unless otherwise noted, the authors and the publisher make no explicit guarantees as to the accuracy of the information included in this book and, in some cases, the names of people, places and organisations may have been altered to protect their privacy. All hyperlinks were believed to be live and correctly detailed at the time of publication.

This book may include references to organisations, feature films, television programmes, popular songs, musical bands, novels, reference books, and other creative works, the titles of which are trademarks and/or registered trademarks, and which are the intellectual properties of their respective copyright holders.

All rights reserved. No part of this publication may be reproduced, stored in a retrieval system, or transmitted, in any form or by any means, electronic, mechanical, photocopying, recording or otherwise, without the prior permission in writing of the publisher.

This book is sold subject to the condition that it shall not, by way of trade or otherwise, be lent, re-sold or hired out, or otherwise circulated without the publisher's prior consent in any form of binding or cover other than that in which it is published and without a similar condition including this condition being imposed on the subsequent purchaser.

A CIP catalogue record for this book is available from the British Library.

ISBN: 978-1-7398543-4-8

Typeset in Sorts Mill Goudy, designed by The League of Moveable Type.

Printed and bound in Great Britain by IngramSpark, Chapter House, Pitfield, Kiln Farm, Milton Keynes, MK11 3LW, United Kingdom.

Cover artwork is Copyright © Stirling District Tourism Ltd., and is reproduced by kind permission of the copyright holder.

Cover design and book design is Copyright © Thomas A. Christie.

Internal photographic images are sourced from the private collections stated in the Image Credits section, which forms an extension to this legal page.

The copyrights of third parties are reserved. All third party imagery is used under the provision of Fair Use for the purposes of commentary and criticism. While every reasonable effort has been made to contact copyright holders and secure permission for all images reproduced in this work, we offer apologies for any instances in which this was not possible and for any inadvertent omissions.

STIRLING LEGENDS

Edited by
Zillah J. Jamieson

Contents

Introduction..Page i

The Wolves of Stirling (Dr Murray Cook)..Page 1
John Cowane: Son of the Rock (Dr Catriona Scott)......................................Page 5
The Black Boy Fountain (Dr David Mitchell)..Page 13
Legends and Lore of Logie Old Kirk (Dr Murray Cook)..................................Page 19
Legends of the Deep: Stirling as a Maritime Town (Dr David Mitchell)..................Page 27
The Beheading Stone of Mote Hill (Dr Thomas Christie)................................Page 37
The Staffman (David Kinnaird)..Page 45
The First Earl of Stirling (Tracey Macintosh)..Page 51
John Damian: The Bird Man of Stirling Castle (Joe Clifford)..........................Page 57
The Barnwell Brothers (Ken Thomson)..Page 65
St Ninians: The Day the Village Exploded (Dr David Mitchell).........................Page 73
Baird and Hardie (David Kinnaird)..Page 83
Christian MacLagan: She'd Make a Jolly Good Fellow (Morag Cross).....................Page 91
Wallace and Cambuskenneth (Nick Brand)..Page 105

Image Credits..Page 109
About Stirling District Tourism...Page 112

Introduction
Stirling: Land of Legends

When a story starts with the words "Legend has it...", we can expect the tale we are about to hear is more than likely going to be a mix of fact and fiction. We can also expect that the story will be well worth listening to. The tales surrounding legends are the ones which are cherished; the ones which are handed on from generation to generation, and faithfully re-told, bringing aspects of our heritage vividly to life.

Those events, occasions and characters recognised as 'legends' have earned that description because of what they mean to so many people. They are the special moments that stand out in history. They are the people that have won our admiration and respect, and it is no big surprise that there are so many associated with Stirling, Scotland's ancient capital. For centuries Stirling has been at the heart of Scotland, and at the heart of the country's history.

Today, legendary characters associated with Stirling welcome visitors on arrival in the city, from whatever direction they are travelling:

- The route for many visitors arriving into Stirling from the south brings them through Bannockburn, where the status of King of Scots **Robert the Bruce** as a national legend was assured when he prevailed over the English army of Edward II in a landmark battle.

- Coming into Stirling from Fife and the east The National Wallace Monument defines the city's skyline, and invites visitors to come and hear the story of the patriot and martyr William Wallace who came to be acclaimed as a Scottish legend.

- The journey from Doune to Stirling brings visitors past a striking statue, looking out across the countryside towards The Trossachs, and which commemorates World War II legend Colonel **Sir David Stirling**, who founded the SAS in 1941.

One of our priorities at Stirling District Tourism is to share the city's incredible heritage with everyone who wants to discover more about what makes it such a special place, so we're delighted that in this Year of Scotland's Stories we can introduce you to this specially chosen selection of legends. You can read about the wolf that saved Stirling from attack, the sculpture which marks the impact of the Black Death in Stirling, and the wealthy merchant who became one of the city's most generous benefactors.

We're sure that you will want to explore Stirling for yourself, to find out more about the city's legends, and discover some new ones along the way.

Whether you're at the start of your journey making plans or you're ready for a break to decide on which legend to tackle next, Legends at the Monument, our lovely coffee house and gift shop at the foot of the National Wallace Monument, is the perfect spot to contemplate your next move. We look forward to welcoming you soon.

Zillah J. Jamieson
Chair
Stirling District Tourism

STIRLING LEGENDS

Edited by
Zillah J. Jamieson

Here in auld days
The wolf roam'd
In a hole of the rock
In ambush lay

The Wolves of Stirling

Dr Murray Cook

There are ferocious wolves all over Stirling… no, don't worry, this is not the next phase of some rewilding project gone amok (though if you do like red kites, beavers and red squirrels you really should visit the wonderful Argaty Red Kite Centre), but rather one of our proud burgh's ancient symbols first recorded in the 13th century. These wolves are always ferocious, defending our city against all comers but gentle to the rightful rulers.

Tradition has it that, during the 9th century, Stirling had been conquered by the Anglo-Saxon Princes Osbrect and Ella. During a Viking raid, the guard at the south gate (presumably the Dirt Raw Port, now under the Thistle shopping mall) had fallen asleep—presumably after a heavy meal and some flagons of local ale! The Viking army had managed to get right outside the city walls without alerting anyone, but they disturbed a sleeping wolf in a cave next to what is now called Wolf Craig. The howling of the wolf woke up the rest of the troops, who chased the Vikings off. The fate of the sleepy guard is not recorded.

A great story, but is it true? There were certainly wolves at this point and while Osbrecht and Ella were real kings of Northumbria, they didn't raid Scotland—let alone conquer Stirling! To be frank, it also sounds a bit too like the honking geese who saved Rome from raiding Celts. We're also really not sure there was a settlement called Stirling in the 9th century as the name probably relates to the lowest crossing point of the river, after which the settlement was named.

But... this period saw several Viking raids on southern Scotland as well as patches of civil war amongst the Scots. In 870 Dumbarton Rock, the ancient core of the Kingdom of Alt Clut, was sacked after a four month siege. In 875 the Viking ruler Thorstein defeated the Scottish King Constantine I at the Battle of Dollar (just a few miles to the west of Stirling) and then used it as bridgehead to conquer Caithness, Sutherland, Ross and Moray. The Dollar Museum has a Viking sword that may have been dropped in the battle and is well worth a wee visit.

Constantine was later killed in Fife fighting another Viking raid in 877, and his successor Aed was murdered by his followers a year later in Dunblane which was then burnt down by the Vikings in 912... Phew! So it seems likely that this legend recorded the memory of some kind of raid, but if not on Stirling then what?

Well, it just so happens that my excavations on the hillfort on the Abbey Craig, under the amazing National Wallace Monument (you know, the big tower thing to the north of Stirling—what do you mean you've not been there yet?!) proves that it was occupied around 900. The fort has two massive ramparts and probably had some form of timber hall on the summit, a place where mead and ale were consumed and poetry and song recounted. It was the immediate predecessor of Stirling and probably built to control the crossing point over the Forth, the most important in Scotland.

So I think it's just possible that the legend garbles a memory of a failed raid on the Abbey Craig fort. However, someone did eventually capture it and it was completely destroyed by fire, perhaps after the Battle of Dollar. The fire was so intense, with temperatures reaching in excess of 1000 degrees centigrade, that the stones began to melt and vitrify. Imagine the whole hilltop on fire for several days, the smoke visible across the whole Forth Valley and the fiery red eye of destruction visible even further at night. A statement of awesome destructive power and regime change. Unfortunately we don't know who was defending and who was attacking… but certainly Stirling's wolves will have howled!

* * *

Dr Murray Cook is a well-known figure round Stirling, where he is the Council's Archaeologist. Murray has published over 50 articles and books about various aspects of Scottish history and archaeology, including four books on Stirling. He writes a weekly column for the *Stirling Observer*, runs night classes at Forth Valley College all about Stirling's past and can often be found down a hole somewhere! Murray also runs Rampart Scotland, a training and research organisation that provides archaeological training for students and tourists. Additionally, he regularly undertakes tours and community excavations round Stirling.

John Cowane: Son of the Rock

Dr Catriona Scott

I am John Cowane and, like all those born within Stirling's ancient boundaries, I am known as a Son of the Rock. However, this nomer is not merely metaphorical but also quite literal as is evidenced by the cold, hard strata of my life. In my many roles, as prentice, penitent, privateer, politician, philanthropist, patron and prisoner, I have undergone a process of self-inflicted petrification. Herein is the story of my fault lines and fractures, laid bare.

Prentice

Named after the Baptizer, John, meaning "graced of God", my birth in 1570, into the prominent Protestant Cowane family, was indeed distinguished as my forebears were well-known merchants. Like James VI, the cradle-King born three years prior to my birth, I spent my childhood on Stirling Castle crag. He was born to a thrice wed, thrice widowed Catholic Queen and I into the home of wealthy merchant, Andrew, and his wife, Issobell, in a vennel named after the Virgin Mother: Saint Mary's Wynd.

My grandfather imported honey, prunes, saffron and spices plenishing the royal banquets of James V. Apprenticing in my father's booth on Broad Street exposed me to splendidly exotic indulgences destined for the young King James VI. Learning the weights, measures and values of these vivid oriental acquisitions and the vicarious journeying to foreign climes were lessons in mathematics and geography which made my grammar school education pale.

Penitent

My royal contemporary was installed not a stone's throw away, at the castle. In 1611, in the wake of the Reformation, he commissioned a translation of the Bible, employing scholars, clergymen, church officials and rebellious Puritans. His authorised version not only aligned an increasingly Calvinistic Scottish church with English theology but established his divine right as King. In that same year, I experienced similarly antagonistic dealings with the kirk. Although unmarried, I was none-the-less cleaved to a beguiling maidservant. As another of my namesakes, the great John Donne, wrote, "Once, and but once found in thy company... And as a thief at bar is questioned... So am I... Yet close and secret, as our souls, we've been... That which betrayed me to my enemy". My indiscretion resulted in a fine from the Kirk Session of £6 for fathering a son out of wedlock. Her transgression, however, warranted not only a fine but also being forced to sit on the threshold of the Church of the Holy Rude in a show of public penance. The indignity overcame her but, like Orpheus, I could not bring my Euridice back from the underworld. I craved the assistance of the mighty Spirit and formidable God, "*Possente spirto, e formidabil nume*", and knew I had been bewitched. I therefore renounced the entanglement and remained a bachelor. The child, having no father to train him in trade, did not follow in the family line of merchantry and, being no Napier, was without a grasp of arithmetic to manage his finances. Instead, he relied on my charity while I lived with my sister, Agnes, as pious as a Pope.

Privateer

Stirling was a growing trade hub. Vessels navigating from the east along the River Forth carried goods and people, and so I invested in shipping. A third-generation merchant, trading with the Dutch, I negotiated on behalf of the Convention of Royal Burghs regarding overseas trade of domestic goods such as fish, coal, salt, wool and hides. And, rather than commissioned ships returning to Europe empty, I saw that they were filled with privately sourced goods, a practice which was, at best, unlicensed ingenuity and, at worst, piracy. Call it what you will, my wealth allowed me to lend money to merchants and purchase considerable dwellings about town.

Politician

In time, I naturally assumed my place as a burgess of the guildry which not only regulated trade but also dictated who traded. We were a force to be reckoned with, both as the town's security outfit and as the enforcers of the church: fining those who contravened civil and religious regulations and using the funds to contribute to the national military. I was made Dean of the Guild and given the privilege of wearing the guildry ring, symbolising honesty and integrity: paramount characteristics befitting the merchant class. I even became a member of the Parliament of Scotland. Without wishing to seem parsimonious, I do consider my dealings to have been upright. The eviction of non-paying tenants is fair to my own pocket, after all.

Since the days of David II, of the House of Bruce, we merchants were freemen and, unlike the unfree craftsmen, had "the free liberty of buying and selling". The quotidian discord this created was, to some extent, assuaged in 1699 when the incorporated trades were given leave to trade by means of payment of a capital or annual sum.

Philanthropist

My life ended in 1633 but not before I had beseeched my brother and heir, Alexander, to endow portions of my wealth to the city. As I lay on my deathbed, my executor noted my bequests to numerous charities, including 500 merks to the Holy Rude, the source of my youthful reprimand and my adult allegiance. Even in death, my zeal for the betterment of the town, and the furtherment of its people, was principal. Since the tailor, Robert Spittal, founded a hospice for the poor in 1530, there had been multiple outbreaks of plague and Stirling knew the reality of its being named after strife. Therefore, the greatest sum was 40,000 merks, given for the building of "ane hospital or almshous" which would provide a dozen elderly merchants succour should they be unable to support themselves. The records of the Merchants' Guild recorded that I had made this bequeathment "to the glorie of God and out of the love [for] this burghe…" The surfeit of needy guildbrothers was such that I had stipulated the King's Authorised scriptures of Saint Matthew be inscribed on the lintel-stone, "For I was an hungry, and ye gave me meate: I was thirstie, and ye gave me drinke: I was a stranger, and ye tooke me in: and ye clothed me: I was sicke, and ye visited me". This was to be a Christian charity and a civic institution to maintain honour for the burgessfolk, managed by a trust and overseen by patrons from the town council, the guilds and, naturally, the kirk.

Patron

Work began at the 'Top o' the Town': an elevated position at the south-west side of the crag, near to the old spittal and just off none other than St John Street. The building was to be monumental and, like its benefactor, was built on underlying rock. Royal master mason John Mylne set to work on a two-storey building with crowstepped gables built in the Scottish Renaissance style with Dutch-influenced detail. The almshouse was opposite the Holy Rude, and adjacent to the Old Town Cemetery and, during an epidemic in 1645, the former became a conduit for the latter. The gardens showed our trade-links, as fruit trees, roses, almonds bushes, flowers and herbs were transported from Holland. The grounds offered panoramic views of the Gargunnock Hills to the south-west and the mountain peaks of Ben Lomond, Ben Venue and Ben Ledi to the north-west. Designed for taking constitutionals, and growing vegetables and herbs, they were later refashioned for recreation, boasting Dutch-style parterres of box hedging and even a bowling green.

On the principal elevation in the north of the courtyard still stands its centrepiece: a four-storey bell tower containing a statue of myself. I am eternally silent, petrified in the Gorgon's gaze and, unlike my scriptural namesake, who cried in the wilderness and witnessed the holy dove come down from an open heaven, all that descends and alights on my shoulder are itinerant pigeons. In troubled times, I have seen the building be commandeered by Cromwell's troops besieging the castle, become a barracks during civil unrest, be transformed into an epidemic hospital during plague and, in better ones, being remodelled for use as a school and a library.

Prisoner

My legacy is carved in the spittal's sandstone mullions, cornices and strapwork and in the gardens' carved balustrades and sundial. And I stand, like old Lot's wife, a megalithic monument to patronage. My heart is no more flesh than when I lived, stonehearted towards the plight of the needy: my tenants, my lover, my son. So animated was I by the accrual of wealth and importance of status, that now I am become an inanimate memorial with a heart as cold as my monogrammed gravestone in the kirkyard. Most, upon death, are transposed to the heavenly realms: a life eternal in glory with their Maker yet I have effectively carved my own destiny: a rigid purgatory for the expiation of my sins. My past elevation through pitiless statute has now encased me with a different kind of stature and I am imprisoned.

Yet, at the turn of each year, God, in His graciousness, grants my spirit merciful redemption. Temporarily freed from my bonds, I become flesh again, descend and take my place among the brethren in the courtyard, as they sing goodbye to the old year and greet the new one with customary dancing. Then, all too soon and before the dawn of Ne'er's Day, I return to my pedimented niche, revert to my original state and wish I had known more of the joys of liberation outwith the confines of the kirk, the guildry and now stone. I am a fixture in the street-names and buildings of Stirling but also a part of the cold fabric. I am John Cowane, but you can call me "Auld Staneybreeks", the one who is set in stone: a true Son of the Rock.

* * *

Dr Catriona Scott graduated with a BA Honours in Scottish Literature from the University of Stirling and a doctorate from the University of Edinburgh School of Scottish Studies where she was also awarded the Grierson and Sloan Prizes for Scots poetry and song. During term-time she tutors undergraduate and postgraduate students across Scotland in Study Skills and, in the summer, teaches Advanced English to international students attending summer school at St. Andrews University. Having been a ghost writer (with many books not to her name!) she is thrilled to be releasing her first children's book with Extremis Publishing in 2023.

The Black Boy Fountain

Dr David Mitchell

The beautiful fountain at Allanpark is one of our most recognisable landmarks—ask any local and they will likely tell you a tale of commemoration to the victims of a plague that wiped out most of the town. They will certainly tell you the water jets used to be much higher (fair enough, really), and perhaps might tell you that the cherub on top of the fountain danced around the fountain at Hogmanay (which I suspect was someone getting confused with John Cowane's statue doing likewise at the Guild Hall).

I became interested in Scottish architectural ironwork some 30 years ago, but could never make sense of the fountain and its story—a key problem being that Neilson and Co were not known for making such work. In fact, I could find nothing else like this made by them. Until very recently, I started to think there was something in the legend after all and decided to have one final push to try and understand the history.

The starting point was the firm's name, beautifully cast into the bottom of the main pedestal supporting the bowls.

Messrs Neilson and Co. moved to Hyde Park Street as Kerr, Mitchell and Neilson in 1837, as Kerr, Neilson and Co. in 1840, and Neilson and Mitchell in 1843. Walter Neilson and James Mitchell dissolved their partnership in 1847 at Hyde Park,

Finnieston and London; the business then carried on by Neilson under the name of Neilson and Co. again. After various permutations, Walter Neilson left the firm in 1884 and set up as Clyde Locomotive Works. In 1903 they merged with several other firms to become the North British Locomotive Co., prolific manufacturers and world-wide exporters of locomotives. The North British Company remains well-known for its prolific high quality output to every corner of the globe. Walter Neilson was the eldest son of James Beaumont Neilson, inventor of the hot blast in 1828 which revolutionised the Scottish iron business.

These were engineers and, in the 1830s, the explosion in popularity of ornamental ironwork had not yet happened—the Great Exhibition of 1850 was some years in the future.

When such a structure was cast in a foundry in this period, the patterns used to create the sand mould in which the molten cast iron would be poured would be timber—the cherub possibly made in clay or plaster to make the sculptural work easier. I am describing him as a cherub rather than a 'putti' although you could spend hours arguing back and forth on that one. Generally this pattern would be used for making multiple castings—the fountain likely appearing in a catalogue to recoup the costs of the pattern over time. Our fountain was a one off, which is very unusual—perhaps they made it and then decided the architectural work was not for them?

There must be somewhere tucked away in some Council Minutes some explanation for all of this, I thought—books and the like repeated the same stuff over and over on the plague. We are fortunate, however, that Stirling has had several newspapers published over time and something like this would surely be recorded…

So after some digging, it would appear our fountain is indeed special but perhaps not for the reason we had thought… let us back up a little.

The fountain was not made for Stirling at all, but was made for a special event in Glasgow in 1849. That event was the visit of Queen Victoria, who arrived by ship on the Clyde on August 13th after visiting Ireland by steamer. The City undertook much work to welcome Victoria to the city—this included a 70ft triumphal masonry arch (designed by J.T. Rochead of Wallace Monument fame) and a decorative spray fountain.

The *Glasgow Herald* describes the fountain, '*A beautiful fountain of cast iron, constructed at the Hyde Park Foundry will be placed either at the foot of South Portland Street or at the South end of the Broomielaw Bridge. It will consist of a colossal youth at an elevation of about 20ft from the ground, throwing the jet through a cornucopia, which in its descent falls into one tazza, from thence into a second and lastly a receiving basin.*' The pipework and water was to be supplied by the Gorbals Gravitation Water Company, and its proposed location beside the Clyde made by Hydepark Foundry. As a decorative ornamental feature at that time it would also be odd for it to have been black—this is largely a 20th Century fiction that ironwork was black—but it appears ours was indeed black from early days.

Early in 1849, the *Stirling Observer* notes that a group of wealthy Stirling residents had lobbied the Council with a proposal to have three fountains or *"jets d'eau"*. One would be placed at the top of Queen Street, another on the site of the old cross at Broad Street and the third on the waste ground where the road splits towards Kings Park and St Ninians.

Stirling Council must have purchased the fountain for Stirling, and it was installed before the year end. The story of the black boy being installed to commemorate plague victims does not appear until the early 20th Century, and whilst the plague was devastating this is not connected to the fountain directly. The erection of fountains to celebrate the supply of clean drinking water was much more common and it was for this reason James Chrystal, Dr Forrest, W. Rankin, John Sawers and Alex Boyd represented 'the most wealthy and respected of the community' to lobby the Town Council meeting to install three fountains in celebration of 'a constant source of water for the town'.

In 1852 the 'ingenuity of Messrs Lochend and Munro—brassfounders' was employed to modify the fountain to have a more ornamental appearance. New jets were fitted to imitate the Prince of Wales feathers and 'other fantastic appearances'. The newspaper was in a state of wonderment for the fountain itself, but again highlighted 'the miserable looking railing that surrounded it'.

Quickly becoming a much-loved landmark, in 1854 concern was expressed at the plight of such a young naked boy in the depths of a Stirling winter. Some youngsters who had been out guising at Hogmanay felt sorry for the young man shivering amongst the ice and 'with an enormous deal of labour scrambled to the top of the fountain and placed upon the black boy a mutch (bonnet) and a bed gown'. The correspondent continued that 'one of our townsmen, passing the fountain in a condition rather merry than wise considered the alteration a change for the better, uttering "Aye lad—if ye winna put your sark on for shame's sake yell hae to do't for the cauld o eh man isna it awfu weather?"' It is not recorded if he received a reply...

In 1943 the fountain was subject to attention in the *Stirling Observer*, where 'JW' noted it was being used as a short cut to the cinema and public convenience (a wonderful cast iron pissoir by the Sun Foundry of George Smith and Co.) and the bulbs that had been planted were destroyed. The cause of this was the removal of the railing referenced in 1852 (!) for the war effort. 'Stirling has been stripped bare of railings!'

Another writer titling himself 'rub it off' bemoaned that the lamp standard lighting the fountain had been painted in oil paint without the addition of 'driers' in the mix (which made the paint harden), so he had been left with a large stripe on his new coat !

A response was forthcoming recording that 'at one period of the boy's life he misbehaved himself so much so that the "unco guid" raised a huge hue and cry over his misconduct. A local wag of some standing, after a night on the town, appreciated the humour and securing a ladder, reached the offending boy and slipped a little sark (vest) over his nakedness. This episode caused no end of good natured chaff for days.'

The fountain has been 'restored' three times in the past twenty years, and is once again operational. The quality of the casting is excellent, and it is nice to identify its origins—our little cast iron boy once gazed down on Victoria and Albert above hundreds of thousands lining the streets of Glasgow, taking early retirement in a rather quieter setting. Maybe it is time that his true story became the legend?

* * *

Dr David Mitchell is Director of Cultural Assets at Historic Environment Scotland and responsible for some of Scotland's most treasured places, collections and archives. He has lived in Stirling for 40 years and is Chair of the Smith Art Gallery and Museum (Scotland's best wee museum!) and a Trustee of Stirling District Tourism. He is proud to be from Stirling, and loves to explore its rich history.

Legends and Lore of Logie Old Kirk

Dr Murray Cook

One of Stirling's most overlooked little jewels is the tiny, ancient Logie Old Kirk, nestling in the slopes beneath the eastern Ochils. It was saved from rampant ivy over a decade ago by the hard work of Joe and Eleanor Young, who formed the Friends of Logie Old Graveyard Group to repair and manage it. I have the honour to be the current chair, and I urge you to go and visit. At no other place in Scotland can you combine Picts, Saints and Vikings with red squirrels, red kites and roe deer! It's also a perfect start to any number of gentle walks and rambles, with spectacular views back to Stirling. But don't go at night and certainly don't go alone, for legend also speaks of a Witches' Sabbath and the Devil.

But first some background. Normally in Scotland, Logie is Gaelic for 'hollow', but in a small number of places where the name is associated with an older church we think it really derives from the latin 'locus', which means 'place'... so with a church, this would be 'the holy place'. The Stirling Logie is the most southern one, and we think it was established by the Pictish Royal family in the aftermath of the Battle of Dunnichen in AD 685. This was where the Picts pushed the Northumbrians out of what would become Scotland. After the Picts conquered Stirling, they established a border with the Northumbrians on the Forth and reorganised the churches... hence Logie Old Kirk. This would have been a very significant place, the first church north of the strategic crossing point at Stirling, a place to pray for a safe trip before crossing the border and to give thanks for a safe return.

We think that the person who did all of this was named Serf, and he seems to have become a Saint after his death. There is a mention of a miracle performed by St Serf in the grounds of Aithrey (now the University) in his biography, and to this day miracles are frequently sought during the exams! But what was this miracle? Well, the Saint was wandering about the countryside and some locals approached him to investigate the theft of a sheep (still a big deal in the more rural parts of Stirling). The Saint asked the suspect if he had stolen the sheep… 'no,' he replied in a confident tone. Once more the Saint asked and once again the thief replied 'no'. On the thrice asking, the Saint asked the man to swear on his Bishop's Staff and as the man reached out his nervous, twitching hand… a sheepy bleat came from his stomach. Now the more sceptical amongst you will simply conclude that this was merely a bad case of indigestion, or perhaps some psychosomatic response from the man's guilty subconscious. However, I remain open to miracles, and the protection of St Serf—especially when it comes to Logie and the risk of the Devil… but more on that later on.

So Logie remained an important place for the rest of the 1st millennium AD, and was probably connected to the two hillforts to the north and south of the site: Abbey Craig and Dumyat, both of which were important places between AD 500 and 1000. These two sites were probably Royal Centres used as Kings moved

round their territory. The fort at Dumyat is named after the local tribe the Maeatae, who fought the Romans and raiding Scots from Argyll. The fort at Abbey Craig was probably built to defend Stirling's strategic crossing points from raiding Vikings, and may even have been destroyed in the aftermath of the Battle of Dollar in AD 875. The fort was destroyed in a fiery inferno around AD 900, indeed so intense and furious was this fire that the stones of the rampart began to glow and melt—a process called vitrification. Can you imagine the whole of the hilltop on fire for several days? An awesome statement of power! Famously, Scotland has the highest number of vitrified forts in the world.

The Vikings appear to have settled in the area, and their traditions gradually influenced local burial patterns. There are at least four Hogback burial monuments in the cemetery, one of the highest concentrations in Scotland. These are gravestones built to resemble Norse longhouses, and were an indication that Logie was still an important place. Such was the significance of the place that it may even have been visited or certainly marched past by William the Conqueror during his invasion of Scotland in 1072. Unfortunately two of the hogbacks were smashed up by a stone mason to help repair the boundary dyke—d'oh!—though the broken pieces remain.

The gradual expansion of Scotland south of the Forth into what had been Northumberland, which culminated in the founding of the Burgh of Stirling in 1124 by David I, reduced the significance of Logie and it gradually became a sleepy rural church with an attached school. Unfortunately school teachers were paid even less during the 17th century, and an extra source of income was recording births and deaths. Famously, one teacher had to sue the Church of Scotland as he wasn't getting his fees!

The church and graveyard remained the key focus of the local community until the start of the 19th century, when the owner of Airthey Estate cleared the two villages that used the church—Logie and Blawloan—and even demolished the church, replacing it with the new one down the hill. The graveyard, however, remained in use till very recently and one of the more famous people to be buried there is the impressive-sounding General Sir James Edward Alexander, K StJ, CB, FRSE, FRGS—a Victorian soldier and explorer whose granddad was a Provost of Stirling, who went to the High School, and who lived in Westerton House in Bridge of Allan. His Wikipedia page shows a very impressive set of bushy muttonchops. He fought in or explored Burma, India, Iran, the Crimea, New Zealand, Canada, Portugal and South Africa to name but a few, and wrote several books about his experiences. However, his chief claim to fame now is that he was largely responsible for the transportation of the 3,500-year-old ancient Egyptian obelisk called Cleopatra's Needle from Egypt to London in 1878. The name derives from the fact that the needle was originally in Alexandria, Cleopatra's royal city. The Needle, which was one of three obelisks, had fallen in antiquity and had been gifted to the British by the local Turkish ruler after the British victory over Napoleon, but it was too big to move. In 1868 it was apparently under threat from being blown up, at which point Sir James became interested and lobbied for its removal to Britain. The transportation was an incredible feat of engineering logistics, and was funded by £15,000 from public subscription. However, there was an even greater cost—the transportation vessel got into trouble, and six men lost their lives. The monument is certainly impressive, but was it really worth it? Sir James' actions appear to have protected the Needle from destruction, but should it not really be in Egypt?

Returning to legend: at the end of the 18th century, Logie witnessed a far more serious victory… one involving the Devil himself. The steep craggy peak to the north-east of Logie Old Kirk is known as Carlin's Crag. Carlin is Scots for witch, and tradition has it that suspected witches were either thrown off it (if they flew off it they were witches… if they didn't, they might be dead but were certainly innocent!) or that Witches' Sabbaths were held on it. Now, late one evening a stout and respected member of the community, a kirk elder no less, was returning after a day's grouse and pigeon shooting, no doubt slightly fou' from some celebratory whisky. Looking up at the Crag and shivering, he spotted in the gloaming the unmistakable form of the Devil. Cunningly, Auld Nick had taken the form of a large black dog and was no doubt getting ready to summon his witches for a night wild of revelry. Reacting quickly he put a silver coin in his gun… (well known to be the correct way of killing the Devil!), sighted, slowed his breathing and fired. The Devil collapsed. The victorious elder ran to the minister to proclaim that he had ended the Devil's evil machinations. The next day the two men climbed nervously to the Carlin's Crag to look for a blackened corpse. When they got there all they found was the cold, prone body of a local woman's pet goat. Tradition does not record the woman's thoughts on the loss of her pet goat or whether the elder was allowed to keep his gun! However, perhaps the goat was an accomplice; perhaps he threw himself in front of the silver bullet to protect his evil master and the Devil survives, watching, waiting for a lone visitor. So be very careful if you visit Logie Old Kirk!

* * *

Dr Murray Cook is a well-known figure round Stirling, where he is the Council's Archaeologist. Murray has published over 50 articles and books about various aspects of Scottish history and archaeology, including four books on Stirling. He writes a weekly column for the *Stirling Observer*, runs night classes at Forth Valley College all about Stirling's past and can often be found down a hole somewhere! Murray also runs Rampart Scotland, a training and research organisation that provides archaeological training for students and tourists. Additionally, he regularly undertakes tours and community excavations round Stirling.

Legends of the Deep: Stirling as a Maritime Town

Dr David Mitchell

The river that runs through our town is most often slow and quiet—even when there is lots of water making its way to the sea, it rarely roars. It winds around Stirling in such a convoluted manner that tourists were attracted to visit and gaze upon 'the windings' of the Forth.

When humans appeared on the scene and up to the start of the 20th Century, the river was important as a travel route, a food and water source, and for carrying goods long distances. Go further back still and it was the river and ice sheet that created our landscape, the access point between North and South, and a topography that many were to fight and die to control.

Given thousands of years of use, it is a little curious that Stirling has for the most part turned its back on the river from whence it came, and has in fact forgotten how important the river—and those who sailed upon it—were to those who came before us and how they lived.

Most Stirling people will have some awareness that there once was a harbour in Riverside. They generally would however find it difficult to visualise how busy it was and the scale of some of the ships working the river. They might be even more surprised to learn that the river is tidal right up to the old bridge, or that one of the earliest steam powered passenger services in Europe operated out of Stirling, heading to the East and Edinburgh.

The logboat discovered in the banks of the Forth in 1874 and presently in store at Cambuskenneth Abbey is a remarkable survivor and example of how water was used as a means of transportation. The discovery attracted much attention and also a little sour grapes when someone suggested they had made it in their shed to confuse the situation…

The first mention of a harbour is in the 12th Century, and then commonly in Burgh records from the 16th Century onwards. Water depth has been a long term issue with 'fords' or bands of hard clay and rock needing removed from the river to allow ships with deeper drafts to access the town. At the end of the 17th Century it is recorded that goods had to be transferred to more shallow boats or 'lighters' to gain access. The Shore Road we know now suggests a shore that boats accessed and allowed themselves to rest on the mud banks as the tide fell.

Improvements were made to the quay from 1603–07. In 1843 an Act of Parliament was obtained by the town council to create a body of Commissioners of the Forth Navigation to improve the navigation of the river between Alloa and Stirling. This was to be achieved by charging dues on passengers and cargo coming into Stirling and deepening the shallows and breaching the fords on the ten mile stretch. David Stevenson managed the works to clear the two principal fords in the river and remove large boulders from the fords. The Commissioners also built the quay, wall and steam boat jetty at Stirling harbour, along from the military quay. In the 1920s and 30s, small freighters continued to make the awkward voyage up the windings over the shallow fords, but trade ended with the 1939 war.

Ship building, an industry all the way up the river, began to decline in Stirling in the late 1850s due to the constraints to navigation. James Johnson's yard launched the 500 ton clipper *Stirling* in 1852 and the 1,000 ton *William Mitchell* in 1856.

A town map of 1740 shows a quay adjacent to where the Engine Shed is sited. A later admiralty quay was located north of this position. This pier had a life beyond WWII, as it was used to transport equipment (often torpedoes) between the workshops in Riverside and the munitions stores at Bandeath down the river. The original drawings for this pier reside in Kew Archives.

A report by the Commissioners in 1843 noted that by 1825, vessels of up to 150 tons had reached Stirling on the Spring tides, and that whilst Alloa had 99 vessels of 17,392 tons, Stirling had only 24 of 1,048 tons and three steamers. The harbour saw around 530 arrivals and sailings annually at this point, plus 492 steam ship trips. From 1843 to 1845 the dues collected had risen from 140l to 350l in 1845. The 1858 map shows the new steamboat Jetty built by the Commissioners.

"The port of Stirling, a member of that of Alloa, carries on an extensive trade in grain, of which considerable quantities are shipped from this place; and there is a moderate extent of foreign trade, consisting chiefly in the importation of timber from Norway, and

bark from Holland. The number of vessels registered as belonging to the port is twenty-two, varying from fifty to 350 tons in burthen; of these, two are employed in the foreign trade, and the others in the coasting-trade, and to ports within the United Kingdom. The harbour is formed by a bend in the Forth, and has a good quay for the loading and unloading of vessels; but the navigation of the river is much impeded by shallows, which retard the approach of vessels of great burthen, and a plan is now being carried out for deepening the river, and consequently improving the trade of the port, and promoting the prosperity of the adjacent district."

(A Topographical Dictionary of Scotland.
Originally published by S Lewis, London, 1846.)

And so to Stirling's little known claim to fame…

The Comet of Henry Bell was the first regular passenger steamer service in Europe. Built in 1812 by John Wood of Port Glasgow, Bell's ship was internationally important and operated in the Forth for a very short time—never reaching Stirling, but running from Edinburgh to Alloa where she caused a sensation. Bell died in poverty, but is internationally recognised for his achievement—he happened to have a guiding hand in Stirling and steam navigation too.

On the 9th of June 1814 local man Dr Lucas recorded, soon after Henry Bell's *Comet* was on the Clyde:

"*A steam boat that was built at Kincardine and intended to run as a passage boat between the town and Leith, came up to the shore, but the debut was rather unfavourable, for instead of running up by means of the steam engine with which it is furnished, it had to be towed up with horses and men.*"

This was the first steam boat to berth at Stirling—'the SS *Stirling*' is the earliest surviving steam ship registration, that of the *Comet* the year before having been lost in a fire. The *Stirling* was a pioneering vessel, as was the service and its operation. She was only the second steam vessel to be built on the East Coast, and amongst the first in Europe.

The *Stirling* was built in the Kincardine shipyard of John Gray for the Stirling Steamboat Co. She was 68 foot long with a 15 foot beam and 69 tons with a square stern. She was owned by a group of thirty seven individuals, allocated one or more sixty fourth shares. They consisted of 23 Stirling merchants, two of whom were already partners in business; two soapboilers; a wright and two butchers, all from Stirling; along with two tanners from St Ninians and one from Bannockburn; a Glasgow merchant; Henry Bell (owner of *Comet*)—described as engineer of Helensburgh Baths; an Alloa wright; an Edinburgh merchant; John Gray, her Kincardine builder; and John Henderson, the first master.

An account of 1874 by Dr Duncanson at the Alloa Society of Natural Science and Archaeology provides a useful perspective. He describes her as a small boat, without covers to the paddles which led to those travelling sometimes getting wet. She had a vertical engine, with the crank driving the paddles via cogs. He also noted that the ship had a flywheel which 'revolved with an interrupted whirring noise', with the upper half of the flywheel exposed above the deck.

This single-masted ship was finished with a highlandman for a figurehead. She worked the Forth along with her later sister ship *The Lady of the Lake* until 1820, when she left for the Caledonian Canal where she ran part of a service from Inverness to Glasgow. Henry Bell operated the *Stirling* steamship on Loch Ness, running between Inverness and Fort Augustus, before the Caledonian Canal was opened from sea to sea in 1822. Thomas Telford was also a partner. Once the final section of the Canal was in service, the *Stirling* was able to connect with the Fort William to Glasgow sailings operated by *Comet II*—enabling a direct steamer connection between Glasgow and Inverness.

Dr Lucas recorded in his diary in July 1814: '*The Steamboat went to Alloa with above 50 passengers in her in order to Attend the Burgher Sacrament and returned again with them on the evening.*'

In May 1816: '*The Old Steam boat that was first set agoing has been repaired and is again set on foot to run between Stirling and Newhaven, near Leith, she has got a new Steam engine put into her.*' On 1st June 1817 he noted that '*The Old Stirling Steam boat began for the Season to go between the Shore of Stirling and Newhaven near Leith, but 'tis reported that her Machinery is often going wrong.*'

In July 1819: 'The Boiler of a steam boat, called the Stirling, burst off Grangemouth, whereby nine persons were very much hurt and Scalded, by the Steam. The Boiler was of Cast Iron, and not of Malleable Iron as all the boilers of the Engines of steam boats generally are now constructed.' The *Stirling* did not operate over the winter.

The *Stirling* was lost in Inverscaddle Bay in Argyll on January 17th 1828 when strong winds blew her onto the shore after the engine failed with one person drowned and 29 others dragged onto shore with ropes. A butler in service with Macdonald of Clanranald drowned, and the colourful Highland chief, Alasdair Ranaldson Macdonell of Glengarry, died later that day of his wounds after jumping from the ship.

The SS *Lady of the Lake* was introduced in August 1815 as sister ship to the *Stirling*, and much faster. She was 60 tons with a crew of four. 'The *Lady of the Lake*, 65 feet keel, 16 feet 4 inches beam, having an engine of 20 horses' power.' Her original engine was by James Cook, Engineer of Tradestown in Glasgow, who was also one of her owners along with John Bryse, spirit dealer; Andrew Hunter, merchant; Lewis McLellan, candle maker; all of Glasgow. She had copper boilers and was noted for her power. She was built at Kincardine by John Gray. On April 8th 1820 she was used to transport 15 men who were part of the radical uprising and captured at Bonnymuir to Edinburgh Castle, returning to Stirling on the 20th. The vessel was lost in 1843.

The potential to make money from passengers who might be on board for 4–7 hours was lucrative—particularly for the steward. Salmon was served in season, and at one point things got a little out of hand when it was found illicit whisky was finding its way on board and being sold to passengers—some even suggesting that journeys were extended when the party really kicked in, in order to make more money from the passengers.

The Quayside buildings were demolished in 1938 and *The Scotsman* noted that even thirty years previous visitors and holidaymakers from Leith to Stirling kept the harbour busy. The buildings on the harbour were used to collect fares and offer a degree of shelter from the weather.

Numerous other vessels ran the passenger route from Stirling to Granton, including:

SS *Lady of the Lake* (1815) who was used to transport 15 men who were part of the radical uprising and captured at Bonnymuir to Edinburgh Castle on April 8th 1820, returning to Stirling on the 20th. Sunk in 1843.

SS *Morning Star* (1815) was the competition to the *Lady of the Lake* until they started working together. By 1854 the hull of the ship was for sale in the *Alloa Advertiser* 'lying at Forth Bank, Alloa'.

The SS *Ben Lomond* (1825) is of note as it went on fire en route to Stirling full of passengers—remarkably everyone on board was rescued despite not enough boats being available. She was then sold to Danish owners.

PS *Stirling Castle* (1826) and later broken up in June 1872.

PS *The Victoria* (1834) operated until 1845 when sold to a new owner in Copenhagen, when she was wrecked at mouth of Agger Canal. All crew reported saved.

PS *The Forth* (1837) only operated until 1842, when she was sold to St Petersburg.

PS *Prince Albert* (1840) operated until 1849, when it collided with Alloa Pier and sunk.

PS *Prince of Wales* (1845) ran from Granton to Stirling until sold on—ending up in Russia in 1879.

PS *Stirling Castle* (1884) had telescopic funnels and forward-lowering mast which enabled her to pass under the Caledonian Railway's swing bridge over the river upstream at Alloa. In 1898, *Stirling Castle* was sold to owners in Constantinople, who renamed her ANATOLI, and she was employed on ferry services on the Bosphorus until she was lost during the First World War.

The railway took the passenger traffic from the ships, and the harbour trade shifted to freight—the Council sought to revive the trade in the 1930s, but in 1938 most of the harbour buildings for passenger traffic were demolished. Around 700 tons/yr were being imported in the 1930s, and this steadily declined until the 1950s when trade pretty much ceased. The last decades mostly saw fertiliser being brought in—a sad end to hundreds of years of people using the river for transport.

* * *

Dr David Mitchell is Director of Cultural Assets at Historic Environment Scotland and responsible for some of Scotland's most treasured places, collections and archives. He has lived in Stirling for 40 years and is Chair of the Smith Art Gallery and Museum (Scotland's best wee museum!) and a Trustee of Stirling District Tourism. He is proud to be from Stirling, and loves to explore its rich history.

The Beheading Stone of Mote Hill

Dr Thomas Christie

It's sometimes said that there are so many sites of historical interest in and around the City of Stirling, visitors coming to see them for the first time might just lose their head. And never was that observation truer than in the case of the famous Beheading Stone—medieval Stirling's traditional stone execution block, which is situated at the top of Mote Hill.

Positioned on the north-eastern side of the Castle Rock, Mote Hill is a very ancient place—even by the standards of a city as historical as Stirling. The rocky promontories of Abbey Craig and Mote Hill once protruded into a long-lost sea back in prehistoric times, and for millennia they were the lowermost crossing point of the River Forth (with either outcropping being situated on opposite banks of the river). Today, all the evidence that remains of this once-vast sea is the fossilised remains of the fish and mammals which considered it their home.

Mote Hill was once the location of an ancient Pictish fort dating to some point between the first and second centuries AD, which would have had a commanding view of the River Forth. This fort was destroyed in a fire, which subsequently produced temperatures so fierce that its structure was vitrified; a fact confirmed by archaeologist Dr Murray Cook during an excavation in 2014. He has suggested that one possible origin for the fire may have been that the fort was set alight by Roman occupiers, perhaps seeking to destroy it during the Empire's retreat south. Mote Hill is at the northern tip of the Stirling's Gowan Hills. While this area only became a part of the famous Royal Park (which includes the nearby King's Knot) around the turn of the 16th century, it would later have great significance in that it would be the spot where the Jacobites positioned one of their batteries when besieging Stirling Castle during the uprising in 1746. The siege took place between the 8th January and 1st February that year, when a large Jacobite force faced off against the government garrison under the command of Lieutenant Governor William Blakeney. When word reached the attacking force that the Duke of Cumberland was leading a relief force north from Edinburgh to break the siege, the Jacobites abandoned Stirling and withdrew towards Inverness.

However, Mote Hill's main claim to fame remains the Beheading Stone itself, which is the reason for its unofficial alternative name, 'Heiding Hill.' If you go to visit the stone today, you will find it mounted on a concrete pedestal and securely protected by an iron canopy which extends over it. However, a closer look at its surface will reveal that the axe-head marks still remain from its bloody past. It is thought that when it was still in use, a thick wooden block would have been fixed to the stone to accommodate the head of the person being executed; there are still visible fastening holes in the stone which indicate where this wooden plinth would have been secured. The exact origins of the stone have not been determined, but it is believed that it was used predominantly in the 15th

century for beheadings – a capital punishment which was reserved for those who were found guilty by the Crown of that most serious of criminal charges: treason. Arguably the most famous victim of this stone chopping block was Murdoch Stewart, Duke of Albany, whose execution was recorded as taking place on 24th May 1425. A one-time Regent of Scotland, Murdoch's death was ordered by King James I, who sought justice for the Duke's disorderly stewardship of the country while the monarch was being held prisoner in England over a prolonged period of many years. Murdoch was the grandson of King Robert II, who had originated the Stewart Dynasty, and his death on Mote Hill led to another of its historical nicknames, 'Murdoch's Knowe.' His father-in-law, the Earl of Lennox, and two of Murdoch's sons were also believed to have been beheaded there as a result of the king's retribution.

A decade or so later, in the April of 1437, Sir Robert Graham of Kinpont – the lead conspirator in the murder of King James I—also met a grisly fate at the hands of an executioner on Mote Hill. The monarch had been staying at the Dominican Priory in Perth when he was attacked by assassins led by Graham; though he made an attempt to evade the confrontation by hiding in a drain, he was eventually found and stabbed to death by his assailants. With no widespread support for his traitorous actions, Graham was apprehended in Perthshire for orchestrating the king's murder and taken to Stirling for trial, where he was found guilty of treason and subsequently executed.

Many years later, the ancient Burgh records note that on 16th October 1525, the mysterious Robert Mentecht was beheaded on the same stone. Though Mentecht's occupation and importance to Stirling's society have since been lost to time, the records indicate that he was executed by Willie Forsycht, who ensured that 'the head [was] to be stricken from the body.'

Another historical curiosity surrounding the hill is that it was given yet another name by the Stirling community, 'Hurly-Haaky', on account of a local legend that King James V used the steep gradient of the hill in his youth for sledging. As 'haaky' refers to a cow in old Scots, it seems that he may have used a cow's skull as a kind of rudimentary sleigh to slide down the hill, with its horns used as handlebars. (In later centuries, a horse's skull was more commonly used by children for this purpose.)

While it may seem amazing that such an innocuous-looking monument should have had such a significant part to play in Scottish history, its gruesome function didn't last forever. The Beheading Stone fell into disuse as a means of execution when Stirling's official site of capital punishment moved to Broad Street's Mercat Cross, next to the Tolbooth (which housed the city's prison until the construction of the Old Town Jail in 1847). However, in later years the stone chopping block was preserved as an historical artefact for future generations; its protective enclosure bears a plaque which reads: 'Beheading Stone, Protected by the Public at the Insistence of the Stirling National History & Archaeological Society 1887.' The stone itself was mounted in its current concrete and iron cage by prominent architect John Allan, who lived nearby. Situated high on the hill, it remains a prominent sight for passers-by, not least on account of the two nearby cannons (added by Stirling Burgh Council in the early 20th century) which are clearly visible from ground level.

While the stone's 'rediscovery' in the nineteenth century guaranteed its conservation, thanks to the expedient action of the historians and archaeologists of the time, Mote Hill also has an even earlier claim to popular culture immortality thanks to author Sir Walter Scott being inspired to include it in his famous 1810 narrative poem *The Lady of the Lake*. Due to its popularity at the period of its publication, Scott's work of historical fiction encouraged a wave of Victorian tourism to Stirling and the Trossachs; set in the time of King James V, the text motivated many visitors to come and see Mote Hill for themselves.

Today, the Beheading Stone is a popular destination for visitors who are travelling along the Back Walk around the Castle; first established by William Edmonstone of Cambuswallace in 1724, the path beneath the Castle Rock boasts terrific views of Stirling, with Mote Hill itself offering an exceptional outlook over the River Forth and over towards the National Wallace Monument on Abbey Craig. The Beheading Stone can be accessed via either Crofthead Road or the aforementioned Back Walk footpath, and is only a short twenty-minute walk away from Stirling Castle.

According to Stirling Ghostwalk, the Beheading Stone has another legend attached to it in the form of the White Lady of Rownam Avenue. This mysterious figure has been reported to have materialised randomly at night near the stone, becoming visible to unsuspecting bystanders. However, the account is considered somewhat questionable given the fact that there has never been a record of 'Rownam Avenue' existing in Stirling at any time in its long history, and the only account of the White Lady seems to derive from the Edwardian supernatural investigator and researcher Elliot O'Donnell in his well-known 1912 book, *Scottish Ghosts*. That being said, visits to the top of Mote Hill in the dead of night are still not recommended—though this has less to do with ghostly sightings and more with the very precipitous steps leading up to it, which are best ascended in daylight!

* * *

Dr Thomas Christie is an author and researcher based in Scotland. He has written eighteen books for publishing companies on both sides of the Atlantic on subjects including modern literature, interactive fiction, digital humanities, and popular cinema. Tom and his books have featured in publications and media outlets including *The Smithsonian Magazine*, *Le Temps*, *Times Radio*, *The Digital Bits*, *The Media Education Journal*, *BBC Radio Scotland*, *History Scotland* and *Retro Gamer*. Tom holds a PhD in Scottish Literature awarded by the University of Stirling, and was elected a Fellow of the Royal Society of Arts in 2018. He currently serves as the Director of Extremis Publishing, which has been named Independent Publishing Company of the Year at the Scotland Prestige Awards for 2021/22 and 2022/23.

The Staffman

David Kinnaird

The tale of Stirling's last torturer and hangman, the 18th-century 'Staffman'—a title unique to Stirling—Jock Rankin, is one of the Royal Burgh's best-known legends. It's certainly one of the most frequently repeated, with variations to be found in countless popular printed histories, at the Old Town Jail visitor attraction, and on the long-running Stirling GhostWalk.

Son of an Ayrshire Hangman, Jock's story was included in Victorian raconteur William Drysdale's hugely popular 1897 local history anthology *Old Faces, Old Places and Old Stories of Stirling*—featuring alongside a venerable host of Provosts, Deans of Guild, Castle commanders and worthies with wonderful soubriquets, like 'Humphy Geordie', 'Bummin' Jamie' and 'Maikey Toy'.

In Drysdale's tales, Jock was a garrulous old curmudgeon, who became the frequent victim of local rowdies—'kail runts', as Drysdale called them:

'more frequently found, and... in greater number, in the neighbourhood of Jock's door than of any other of the inhabitants, the spirit of mischief leading [them] to devote more of their time and attention to him, in the hope of greater sport being obtained by reason of his eccentricity'.

In William's accounts Jock is a glorious grotesque, a stumbling, bumbling buffoon—particularly in accounts of the Staffman cat-and-mouse love affair between Rankin and an Irish laundry thief named Isabella Kilconquhar—known to locals, unable to penetrate her Hibernian brogue, as *'Tibbie Cawker'*—thrown into the Stirling Tolbooth for snatching laundry from a clothes-line. Drysdale lingers upon every detail, and, even today, enjoys a justified reputation as an entertaining storyteller—always a reliable source for other scribblers in search of a couthy anecdote or pithy aphorism.

Well, maybe not *quite* so reliable.

His account of Jock's part in the execution of Sarah Cameron, a young woman condemned to hang at the Gallows Mailing (now occupied by the Victorian 'Black Boy' Fountain) is genuinely shocking. It's cited, with William as a trusted authority on local lore, in many books on Crime and Punishment:

'Attending the sad scene were the town officers with their halberts, and one of them, Tom Bone, seeing the dilemma, went deliberately up, and gave the woman's fingers several knocks with his halbert, which caused her to let go, and Rankin succeeded in pushing her off. A good deal of sympathy was expressed for the woman, but Bone's vulgar and inhuman interference incurred the dire displeasure of the juvenile and female portion of the community, and he had to be escorted to a place of safety until the affair blew over.'

Jock's pitiful performance has endured in popular memory.

This is unfortunate—given that the story is almost complete bunkum.

For all his many faults, the calamities accompanying Mistress Cameron's ignominious exit from this world simply *cannot* be attributed to him.

Sarah Cameron is listed in Burgh Records as having been hanged for 'Child Murder' in Stirling, but the date of her despatch is recorded as 29th October 1784—by which time Jock had not occupied the office of Staffman for some thirteen years—and was, most likely, dead for ten of those.

Poor Sarah was most likely despatched by Jock's successor as Staffman, James Cuthill.

Yup, Maister Rankin was neither the 'Last Hangman', nor remotely responsible for his most notorious execution.

Drysdale was a committed antiquarian and passionate populariser of the minutiae of local history. *Old Faces, Old Places and Old Stories of Stirling* is a treasure-trove of riotous reminiscences of Burgh life which might otherwise be lost to us—from Queen Victoria's visits to the opening of the National Wallace Monument. He was supremely 'well connected', but his passion for the quaint and the couthy—for a good tale, well told—often led him to rely far too heavily on unreliable (if entertaining) anecdote. And because of his reputation, few checked *his* facts.

His greatest contribution to Rankin's enduring mythology is his amusing account of Jock's passing from this world.

'One day, and that a Sabbath, a disturbance took place, and Jock, though an old man, determined to give his wife a thrashing. Tibbie had the good fortune to elude him and took refuge in a neighbour's house. Returning to his dwelling, he seized a basin of cold soup, which he greedily drank, but it so happened that a small bone stuck in his throat and ultimately choked him...'

A hangman choking to death? A dish laden with a *soupson* too much of dramatic irony.

According to William, Tibbie returned to the Close just in time to witness her husband's passing:

'with exemplary affection and tenderness [she] tended him in his last moments, and did her utmost to alleviate his sufferings.'

Touching—but, again, complete humbug. Stirling Town Council Minutes for 2nd February 1771 relate a very different, and somehow less satisfying, end to the Staffman's career:

'The Council Considering, that John Rankine the present Staffman, is not only upon occasions when necessity Calls unable to execute his Office, but also that he and his Wife keep a Bad House in the Night-time by entertaining Tinkers and Vagabonds and having quarrels with them to the great annoyance and nuisance of the Neighbourhood. They therefore dismiss him as Staffman, and appoint the Sheriff to give him Ten Shillings Sterling, money for paying the expense of Carrying him and his Wife to Glasgow or elsewhere.'

Yet, somehow, people preferred the former version of the tale, first mention of which is made just two years after his departure—at which time Jock was alive and well, back in his native Ayr.

But, truth be told, Drysdale's accounts can really only bear half the blame for Jock's enduring legacy. The rest is… 'Fake News'.

In the late 19th and early 20th centuries, when William Drysdale enjoyed his greatest success, in print, the Old Town was in serious decline. The Staffman's official residence, 'Hangman's Close', adjacent to the Tolbooth in St John Street, was described by our favourite author as:

'a mere apology for a human habitation, many a stable in the town being said to be more comfortable.'

It was also being used by vagrants as a make-shift doss-house, and had become a focus for the fascinations of local children—descendants, no doubt, of the 'kail runts' who had allegedly plagued Jock.

Aware of the potential danger of this situation, the parents took the safest course they could.

They lied.

Local bairns were warned by peers and parents alike to avoid the gloomy high-walled huddle of the Close, lest they be set upon by Rankin's wraith—his spectre's oft-reported gagging growl, heard echoing through its draughty chambers, explained away as Rankin's eternal effort to dislodge the fatal fowl-bone from his ghoulish gullet.

And, of course, it worked.

Which just goes to show—as Maister Rankin, himself, says every night on the Stirling GhostWalk—you should never let a little thing like The Truth get in the way of a good story.

* * *

David Kinnaird is an actor, writer, historian and folklore specialist with a lasting passion for the mysteries and histories of Stirling's oddest books and crannies—a familiar figure to locals and visitors in his regular guise as the Burgh's notorious 'Happy Hangman', Jock Rankin, and as Creative Director of the Old Town Jail. His abstruse musings can be heard on the popular Patreon podcast, 'Spooks and Bogles'.

The First Earl of Stirling

Tracey Macintosh

The title 'Earl of Stirling' was created in 1633 for an intriguing and colourful character, William Alexander. One of many titles bestowed upon Alexander throughout his lifetime, the title became dormant upon the death of the fifth Earl in 1739.

By 1603 Scotland and England were unified under the same monarch who had moved South; however, Stirling was still a hugely important town in Scotland with its key central position clasping together the highland and lowlands, its bustling port and its history of iconic battles that helped shape Scotland particularly throughout the Wars of Independence. So who was the first Earl of Stirling and how did he come to acquire such an illustrious title?

William Alexander was born in Menstrie Castle in 1567. His father, Alexander Alexander of Menstrie, claimed to be descended from Somerled, Lord of the Isles. This may have had a bearing on the sea faring adventures of William in later life! On his father's death in 1580, he was thought to have spent some time with an uncle in Stirling, continuing his education there, and may have also attended Glasgow University.

An ambitious young man, Alexander's family were linked to the powerful Campbells and when the head of the Campbell family, the Earl of Argyll, invited

Alexander to accompany him to France, Spain and Italy, Alexander jumped at the chance. On returning to London, Alexander was then introduced to King James VI and I by the Earl of Argyll, beginning a long association with the royal court. A celebrated literary figure of the time, he published a number of works including 'Aurora' and 'Doomes-Day' and assisted the King with the translation of 'The Psalms of King David', a copy of which is exhibited in the National Museum of Scotland.

Knighted by James VI and I in 1609 he went on from there to be appointed Secretary of State for Scotland in 1626, an office he held until his death in 1640. On the death of James VI and I in 1625, Alexander remained in favour in the court of Charles I and continued to be a regular at court in London.

An astute politician, Alexander purchased a tower house in 1629 just a stone's throw from Stirling Castle and set about creating a suitable home for his aspirations. The tower house was expanded and rebuilt in Renaissance style and with its prominent position on the road up towards the Castle, the importance of its occupant was in no doubt whatsoever, most likely exactly what Alexander had planned.

Prior to purchasing this townhouse, James VI and I granted Alexander a vast territory on Canada's East coast, Nova Scotia. A key territory for fishing, shipbuilding and transatlantic shipping, French settlers had staked a strong claim to the territory. Undeterred, Alexander sunk the bulk of his own fortune into establishing Nova Scotia as a Scottish outpost. Although today he is known as

the founder of Nova Scotia, his enthusiasm was misplaced and he lost his investment when the area was returned to France in 1632.

There are still some vestiges of Gaelic culture throughout Nova Scotia, and the province's flag remains strongly Scottish—a blue saltire against a white background with the royal arms of Scotland at the intersection of the cross—one of the longest-lasting legacies of the Earl of Stirling in Nova Scotia.

His financial losses in Nova Scotia had a considerable impact on Alexander, perhaps softened slightly when Charles I bestowed upon him the titles of Earl of Stirling and Viscount Canada in 1633.

His losses didn't dampen his sense of adventure and, in 1637, when Charles I arranged to have a large island off the East coast of the USA transferred to Alexander, he dispatched his agent, James Farret, to the island. Farret was arrested, although he did manage to escape. Perhaps thinking better of this new venture, Alexander arranged to sell on the island through Farret, losing out on what is now said to be one of the wealthiest and most expensive neighbourhoods in the world—Long Island!

Although his far-reaching ambitions were evident in some of his overseas endeavours, William Alexander died in London in 1640, far from being the wealthy man his numerous titles and political aspirations might suggest.

One story suggests he was so much in debt by the time he died that his body was smuggled back to Scotland in a barrel of brandy to avoid the debt collectors who may have sold on his body to reclaim some of his outstanding debts. The story continues that, to further foil any persistent debt collectors, Alexander's family had his body buried at midnight in the graveyard at Stirling's Church of the Holyrude just across from his town house.

Alexander's town house passed into the hands of the Campbell family in the 1660s and was renamed Argyll's Lodging. Archibald Campbell, the 9th Earl of Argyll, extended the house and invested in some impressive *tromp l'oeil*, some of which is still visible today in the house's high dining room. Today the house is in the care of Historic Environment Scotland but is not currently open to visitors.

A glimpse through the gate into the courtyard of the house does reveal William Alexander's coat of arms depicting a mermaid, to symbolise his ventures overseas, a first nation person and a beaver, both depicting his involvement with Nova Scotia.

* * *

A well-known face in Scotland's tourist industry, Tracey Macintosh combines her passions for Scotland's history and landscape into presenting the best of Scotland to visitors from near and far in various visitor attractions and events throughout Central Scotland and beyond.

As Stirling Castle's Event Manager for over 18 years Tracey has fond memories of creating breath-taking Scottish themed events against the backdrop of one of Scotland's most spectacular Castles for thousands of guests, both local and worldwide. Since leaving Stirling Castle, as well as contributing to online magazine Discover Scotland, Tracey has set up her own consultancy and supports other Scottish businesses in honing and presenting their tourism products to national and international clients.

John Damian: The Bird Man of Stirling Castle

Joe Clifford

It's hard to imagine today that a little city like Stirling could once have been a pioneering hub for one of the primary technologies of the modern world; for those who do, we often assume that our golden age was in later times and in events of a more global standing. The technology in question? Why, nothing less important than the power of flight itself.

An engineer or a physicist might find a worthy substitute to an airport when they look at the fine volcanic rock at the heart of our town; but while they would assure us that the most important quality it gives in this regard is its lofty height, I can assure you that for the purposes of this next legend, the most important quality of this fine rock is what was once located at its very top.

Imagine if you will, a man, dressed in the finest of medieval garb, pantaloons adorn his thighs, striped and bright, resplendent in yellows and gold. Upon his torso a fine doublet of similar colour, cut so as the wealth of its inner fabrics could be seen by all. Upon his wisest of heads was a bonnet of bright orange velvet, shimmering in the afternoon sunlight which had the effect of silhouetting him against the skyline to the tightly packed crowd of onlookers who had found time in their busy days to follow their king onto the very ramparts of the castle to see what could only be described as magic, or perhaps more worryingly - science.

The wind was warm, blowing gently from the west, the mountains of the southwestern highlands more than visible in the crystal-clear air, for a moment it was as if he felt the change of temperature as a cloud cast its shadow on a mountainside many miles in the distance.

As he strapped his huge wings to his arms (for he would suffer no other to touch the objects for fear they may be damaged by some half drunk brute or halfwit) his eyes glanced downwards, overwhelmed by the vastness of the space between himself and the valley floor, several hundred feet below. For a time his eyes caught sight of falcons beneath him, darting and climbing in the warm afternoon air as they fledged, leaving their nests in the castle rocks quite possibly for the first time, to experience the awesome quality of flight and for the briefest of seconds he felt an epiphany, a shared connection between man and bird that for all its joy, hung awkwardly in the mind of John Damian.

As the time approached and the crowd and king could hold their suspense no longer, the alchemist took one final, shuffling, step towards the edge of the wall, which stood several stories high perched on top of a sheer vertical cliff (which in its day had proven high enough to stand in the way of the likes of Longshanks and his armies). Below this still, at the base of the cliff, was a slope which ran many feet to the valley floor. It was a long, long way down.

Unperturbed, John Damian thought of the falcons, darting in the sun—how easy they made it look.

John Damian, alchemist to King James the Fourth in the early 1500s was a man of many talents, not least persuading the king to part with sums of money. It would appear that John Damian had managed to fulfil the building of a furnace suitable for producing an elixir of life and useful in the pursuits of other crafts, perhaps even turning common metals into gold. His experiments required expensive components which could only be acquired with the patronage and funding of the king and this would likely have been one of the main tasks of John Damian's employment within the royal court, keeping King James on side with his purse at the ready. King James was a regular visitor to his projects and would have kept a close eye on his alchemist—much to the advantage of the alchemist, for in keeping the attention of the king he could be more assured of access to funding.

In order to gain any form of understanding of who John Damian was and why he did the things he did, we really have to see him in context, to think of him in his contemporary setting so we can get a sense of the man when beside his peers. The royal court of King James the Fourth was a fine place, a fine place indeed. It had to be, because it had to fulfil many functions of state. It was more than just the home and entourage of a renaissance monarch, it was a theatre whose function was to fulfil the political will of a nation. It had to be packed with everything and everyone that a government needed to achieve its goals, whatever those goals may be. Over the decades and centuries that the royal court was in and around the city of Stirling the castle played host to choir schools, blacksmiths, stables, ambassadors, lions (yes that's right, big scary things like lions were in the castle from time to time), religious men, scholars, poets and even alchemists.

Against this hectic and diverse backdrop there are several other threads to weave into our royal tapestry. The outward appearance of the royal court was all important, theatre and vanity were everything. If life wasn't hectic enough with hundreds of people crammed into the royal court, we have to remember that as much as possible the image and theatre of daily life had to be measured, well thought out and as perfectly presented as possible. The next issue to remember is diet and drink, in particular the latter of the two. Alcohol to put it mildly was not in short supply, and the king and his court were (in today's words) a very merry bunch with the king at the absolute heart of the show.

With this in mind it was highly advantageous to keep a keen sense of the theatrical and an even keener sense of where the king's attention (and finances) were focused.

Not a great deal has come to light about the early life of John Damian, and it's true that during the fourteen and early fifteen hundreds the courts of the great and the good along with religious communities provided the best source of records, so it goes without much notice that he reaches the limelight once he comes into attendance at the court of King James. Italy or France are the likely front runners for nations of his birth and possibly his greatest moment comes to us in part from a poem written by another courtier—so in addition to being a legend, the man is most definitely mysterious.

We'll probably never be fully certain of why John Damian jumped from the battlements of Stirling Castle in 1507, but we know enough to suggest several likely motivations. In order to gain more financial support and income, John Damian would have had to provide demonstrations of his capabilities both to bedazzle the monarch and to give just cause for the funding, as funding (as it almost always is) was hard to come by and the royal court was a hive of like-minded competitors who all had their unique skills and reasons to need financial patronage from the king. It could well be that, given the inherent difficulties in distilling the elixir of life or turning lead into gold, and with the competition circling around the financial income, John Damian judged the time was right to unveil something remarkable, something which would keep him in the purse of the king and on the tip of the tongues of all who witnessed. The power of flight, or at least a good attempt at it!

John Damian boasted that he would fly to France! And he made it, all the way, to the ground. His fall broken most kindly by a midden, a rubbish heap built up beneath the castle walls over the centuries was just enough to keep our man from death. According to some it took him two days to crawl back into the castle with nothing more than a broken leg to keep his broken wings company. However, the king did indeed show generosity to his alchemist, bestowing upon him a pension to go with his already more than significant gifts. Given his relative success within the royal court of King James the Fourth and the glimpses of his life that were left for us as a result, we can safely say that John Damian holds a legendary status that—even if we wished to—many of us would struggle to attain nowadays. But far more importantly than this, when measured against the rich and ornate tapestry of life in a renaissance royal court, John Damian may well have been quite rightly considered a legend in his own lifetime.

* * *

Joe Clifford has been working in Scottish tourism for 16 years, including a number of years as a guide in Stirling Castle introducing local and international visitors to one of Scotland's most magnificent historic sites.

Now a professional tourist guide with over 10 years experience, Joe brings to life the best that Scotland as a whole has to offer for guests from around the world, although as a local lad he most enjoys showcasing Stirling and all its treasures, both well-known and more obscure. Joe can be booked for a tour through the Scottish Tourist Guides Association.

The Barnwell Brothers

Ken Thomson

Transport services—in their many forms—are something we all rely on, day in, day out. They put produce on the shelves of our supermarkets, they take children to school all across the country, and they make it possible for families to get together for special occasions. They aren't something we would normally associate with revolutions however, but it's no exaggeration to think along those lines when we realise how our lives have been transformed by the development of transport.

When the railways arrived in the 19th Century they brought mobility to millions—and they had a massive influence on the shape of our towns and cities, all across Scotland.

When the possibility of personal transport became a reality for everyone in the 20th Century, the lives of households everywhere were transformed by car ownership.

And of course we've all been living through the 'low-cost revolution' which has opened up the skies and made air travel accessible—and affordable—on a scale which could never have been imagined.

The revolution in air travel is just the latest chapter in a fascinating story—one in which the city of Stirling played its part, thanks to two pioneering brothers whose names would become forever associated with innovations in aviation: Harold and Frank Barnwell.

* * *

It's reasonable to assume that a fascination with 'how things work' was a feature of family life in the Barnwell household, as Harold and Frank's father—Richard—had moved from Lewisham with his wife Ann, to join the renowned Fairfield Shipbuilding & Engineering Co. Ltd. in Govan. By 1889 Richard was managing director of the company, which was revolutionising sea transportation by building the largest and fastest vessels the world had ever seen.

From their home in Balfron, Richard and Ann raised a family of six children (three girls and three boys), and both Harold and Frank entered their father's company as apprentices after completing their schooling at Fettes College.

It was Harold, the eldest son, who founded the 'Grampian Engineering and Motor Company' in a large hut at Causewayhead in Stirling in 1907, with the support of his other brother, Archibald. They were soon to be joined by Frank, who had attended evening classes whilst serving his apprenticeship at Fairfield, and who had graduated from Glasgow University (with a B.Sc. in Naval Architecture and Engineering) in March 1905. Putting both his academic knowledge and the skills he had gained at Fairfield into practice, he spent a year in the U.S.A. where he worked on hull design for a shipbuilding company, and met the Wright brothers.

The brothers' fascination with the potential of aviation soon became their passion—and it wasn't long before they built their first powered aircraft, a single-seat bi-plane fitted with a 7 h.p. Peugeot engine. It was tested in 1908 at Cornton Farm, but it failed to lift off, a result which unfortunately they also experienced with their second aircraft, a monoplane with an airframe designed by Frank, and an engine designed by Harold.

Undeterred by these early setbacks, the brothers persevered, and applied the principles of aeronautics in designing and building a canard biplane to improve their chances of success. This latest aircraft was powered with an engine built by the Humber car company for the Tourist Trophy races, connected by chains to two propellors, and its landing gear was based on the design of nothing more sophisticated than a bicycle.

This was clearly a step in the right direction—and on Thursday 8th July 1909, six years after Wilbur and Orville Wright had completed the world's first controlled, powered flight in North Carolina, history was made when the aircraft took off, with Harold Barnwell at the controls. The brothers' dream of being responsible for Scotland's first powered flight had become a reality, and it had all happened in Stirling, in close proximity to their Causewayhead base.

Whilst that first flight was only airborne for a distance of 80 yards, and although the aircraft was damaged on landing, the brothers headed back to their workshop to rebuild their craft, reducing the wingspan to 45 ft. Further successful trials took place in September 1909, and interest grew as the news of the innovative developments taking place in Stirling spread across Scotland.

* * *

Early in 1910 Frank's life was to change, when he became engaged to Marjorie, one of the children of Lt. Col. Charles Sandes, an officer in the 10th Royal Hussars. Perhaps it was the prospect of being able to enjoy a settled family life with his new wife, or maybe even the news that broke just a few weeks later announcing the death of Charles Rolls (of Rolls-Royce fame) as a result of an accident during a flying display in Bournemouth, which persuaded Frank that he should pursue a less risky career. For all the excitement which it offered—aviation in the early 1900s was certainly a perilous pursuit—Frank returned to Fairfield to further his career in shipbuilding, the sixth (and final) aircraft built at the Grampian workshops in Stirling was designed by Harold alone. A very different machine, it was a single-seat monoplane, with an engine built by the company itself, and with such innovative features as a windscreen for the pilot! The year 1911 wasn't very old when Harold took to the skies on 11th January, making the longest flight of any Scottish aircraft or pilot up until that time, and on 30th January he was successful in reaching a height of 200 ft. For these accomplishments he was presented with the J.R.K. Law prize, presented by the Scottish Aeronautical Society.

By August of that year the scene of action had moved from Causewayhead to Blair Drummond, where Harold completed further flights—taking off and landing at Cambusdrennie Farm. The last flight to be reported at that location was on 13th October 1911—and from that point onwards the two brothers were destined to have their own individual careers, each reflecting the significance and impact of those early days when they worked together in Stirling.

By September 1912 Harold had qualified for his Royal Aero Club certificate in a Bristol bi-plane, and he subsequently joined the new Vickers School of Flying—his skills being put to good use as an instructor and as a test pilot. It was in the latter role that he was to tragically lose his life—on 25th August 1917, whilst test flying the prototype Vickers F.B.26 Vampire night fighter at Joyce Green, in Kent.

At the inquest into Harold's death it was recorded that in the course of his flight he had 'looped the loop' several times, and that he eventually attempted to 'roll' his aircraft. Having successfully completed his first spin, it was during his second attempt that his machine crashed to the ground at a speed estimated to be between 150 and 200 miles per hour.

Harold was laid to rest in the parish churchyard at St. Mary's, at Byfleet in Surrey, his grave marked by a simple inscription, showing the date and location of the death of an aviation legend.

***

Although Frank had returned to the world of shipbuilding, he no doubt followed his brother's pursuits and achievements, and whether it was sibling rivalry or simply his love for the adventure of flying, within a year he had decided to pursue a career in aviation. December 1911 saw him taking up a position with the British and Colonial Aeroplane Company, an organisation which would become the Bristol Aeroplane Company Ltd. in 1920, with over 3,000 employees in its plants at Filton and Brislington.

Having joined the firm as a draughtsman, he was soon designing aircraft, and even as all of the horrors of World War I were being experienced he joined the Royal Flying Corps, so that he could qualify as a pilot. Whilst he logged many hours of service with No. 12 Squadron, including hundreds of hours flying solo in more than 30 different types of aircraft, it was his talents as a designer which were most in demand, and he used his experience from being in the cockpit to make a valuable contribution to the Bristol company's work.

Frustrated by the uncertainty which followed the cessation of fighting in 1918, Frank sought experience overseas, and served two years as a Squadron Leader, Technical, in the Royal Australian Air Force, before returning to England in October 1923, and re-joining Bristol as Chief Designer.

A prodigious designer, Frank contributed to over 150 aircraft designs over the course of a 26 year career at Bristol, but he never lost his love of flying—a passion which sadly cost him his life. Having made a successful first flight in July 1938 in a single-seat monoplane which he had designed and built himself, his second flight in the aircraft on 2nd August 1938 was to end in tragedy, as the machine stalled and went into a spin, with Frank losing his life in the accident.

For his widow, Marjorie, the pain of loss was something she would experience again during World War II with the loss of their three sons—Richard, John, and David, all of whom were serving as pilots with the RAF.

* * *

There's something which sets true legends apart from others.

They have courage.

They have determination.

They have vision—and these are all qualities which Harold and Frank Barnwell had in abundance. For their contribution to aviation, and to the story of Stirling, may they be long remembered.

* * *

Notes

An original wing strut from the aeroplane in which Scotland's first powered flight was made is on display at the Stirling Smith Art Gallery and Museum.

The accomplishments of the Barnwell brothers are commemorated by a sculpture which stands at the northern end of the Causewayhead Road in Stirling (close to the site of their workshop), and by a woodcarving on 'The Wallace Way', the trail which leads to The National Wallace Monument, on The Abbey Craig.

* * *

Having studied Transport & Physical Distribution at The University of Northumbria, Ken Thomson embarked on a career in transport—spanning the bus, rail, and short-sea shipping sectors, before focusing on travel and hospitality, where he gained experience with international brands including Radisson and Hilton.

From 2004 to 2020 Ken was a member of Stirling District Tourism management team, and since 2006 he has been teaching in Stirling Management School (at The University of Stirling).

Ken is a past Chair of The Chartered Institute of Logistics and Transport (Scottish Region), and is an advisor to the Institute's UK Board on Education and Professional Development.

St Ninians: The Day the Village Exploded

Dr David Mitchell

St Ninians (earlier known as Eccles / Egglis / Kirktown and St Ringans) was a village long before it was consumed by the expansion of the town, and still retains identifiable features that hark back to that point.

The old church tower is a recognisable landmark for miles around and, aside from the clock chimes, it presents a quiet and peaceful setting. Pause for a minute and you will notice something rather odd in that this is not a stand alone tower—there are some remnants of outer walls that indicate a larger structure. Whilst hard to visualise now, this was one of the most important medieval churches in Scotland—a very significant site in the early development of Christianity in Scotland, yet largely overlooked. It would be simple to assume that decay and subsequent demolition led to the current site as we see it—but this was actually the result of a single catastrophic event: the day that St Ninians exploded.

St Ninians was a place of worship from an early period, but first recorded in the 12th Century when at Edinburgh Castle, Alexander I was witness to an agreement on the the relationship between the church of 'Eccles' and the chapel at Stirling Castle. The parish of St Ninians was large, extending into the Carron Valley and towards the Gargunnock Hills. A rededication of the church by Bishop David de Bernham of St Andrews took place on 16 August 1241. At the Reformation the church sat under the control of the abbey of Cambuskenneth and 'their fruits' were accounted for within the total revenues of the monastery.

By the early 18th Century the church was in disrepair, and in 1721 the architect Robert Henderson reconfigured and rebuilt the church with the tower as we see it now rebuilt in 1734. The remains of the Chancel (altar area) are much earlier and can still be seen. A clock was introduced in 1735, funded by the sale of 23 trees(!), and the bell was rung at 5am and 8pm until the First World War.

There are no accurate images of the original church yet found, but the footprint of the building has been used to suggest what the church may have looked like. The church was extensive, the aisle described as *'fifty foot in length, and 46 ft in breadth and built 1722 at the expense of 500 L sterling'*. The Jacobite fan in the Smith Art Gallery and Museum is the only known representation of the church.

In times of war, churches often found use as secure locations for accommodating troops and storing equipment, and St Ninians Kirk was no different. In 1651 Cromwell had marched from Falkirk to within a mile of Stirling, where he took refuge in St Ninians Kirk from a wild storm. Our story starts one hundred years later in 1745 as the Jacobite uprising started to crumble. Charles Edward Stuart arrived in Stirling on the 4th of January 1746 where he took up residence at Bannockburn House, home of Sir Hugh Paterson and his niece Clementine, where he summoned the Town Council on the 5th and they handed over the keys to the town on the 6th. The rest of January saw him claim victory at a battle in Falkirk and then laying siege to Stirling Castle until he reluctantly agreed his

army could not face Cumberland and the retreat northwards scheduled for the 1st of February.

The Jacobites had used the Kirk as their magazine—storing their gunpowder but also cannon and other weaponry. Things were happening quickly, and what happened next still seems rather hazy. What we know for certain is that the magazine caught light either on purpose or by accident and exploded, killing eleven people and blowing out all of the window glass in the village and some in Stirling. The explosion was extremely large—Lord George Murray who was lodged in the town noted 'I believe the like of it was never heard of'.

The Kirk could not contain such a blast and was largely destroyed, with the remarkable exception of the tower which remained largely intact, and remains of the Chancel. Such was the scale of destruction that there was no serious consideration given to re-building and the old Kirk was abandoned, and a 'temporary' church was built across the road which eventually became a permanent home to the congregation to this day.

The Government were quick to assign blame to the Jacobites, and they in turn seemed a little confused themselves—so what actually happened? To find out, we have to peer through the gloom of 18th Century 'spin'.

From the government perspective :

The author of a pro government pamphlet in 1745-6 set out to provide *'Account of the great distress brought by the Rebels on the loyal parishioners of St Ninians, near Stirling'* to demonstrate the explosion was an act of barbarity.

The pamphlet suggests that the Jacobite Captain had rounded up ten local men at night and the following morning they were instructed to take 9 barrels—each of eight Scots gallons—and lay a trail of gunpowder from the magazine in the church to the front door and out into the church yard. Within the church there remained over 100 barrels. Outside, the soldier fired his musket attempting to light the trail and missed—his colleague did likewise and *'kindled the train, and the whole fabric of the Church was instantly blown up'*.

Both men were killed instantly and another two soldiers nearby were wounded. Two local men who had carried the powder also died—yet another man was blown 200 yards from the church *'yet was wonderfully preserved'*.

This account said the initial misfire saved many lives—as the church had local people inside collecting tent cloth that would otherwise be burned, the shot prompted them to flee the church. Eight further locals had died in the church.

The leaflet recorded a Rebel Captain had advised his landlord that he had been ordered by the Colonel of the Artillery to explode the magazine, but he could not do such a thing to a church. It was noted that the shot that ignited the powder came from a servant of the Colonel who was watching from a distance.

The press recorded that 'a great part of the baggage of the Rebels lay under the rubbish of the church of St Ninians to which they immediately went and on searching it found many tents, cloth, linen and other valuable things of their plunder from England. In some Jacobite houses in St Ninians they found many bags of powder and a great number of gunlocks. At the back of the church they found an 18 pounder on a fine French carriage.'

An account of the ordnance found at Stirling was recorded in detail by the military before being despatched to the south and beautifully recorded.

From the Jacobite perspective :

In his journal, Minister John Cameron noted that Lochiel—who had been wounded at Falkirk—was injured and in a horse carriage with Mrs Murray (of Polmaise) passing St Ninians when it passed on the main street. They just escaped being hit by falling masonry, and she was thrown down into the road. Cameron noted that it surely must have been an accident, as Locheil would have known this was going to happen or his men would have cleared the area.

Another account suggests the Prince had also just passed through the village.

A more recent discovery provides the testimony of a Jacobite prisoner shortly before his execution. Christopher Pattenson wrote to the Duke of Newcastle confirming the execution of rebel prisoners at Penrith on 28 October 1746: John Roobottom; Philip Hunt; Valentine Holt; Andrew Swan; James Harvey; David Home and the Priest Robert Lyon. The dying speeches of Home, Roobottom and

Lyon were taken from the prisoners after they read them to the crowd, and were sent to the Duke of Newcastle and have found their way to the National Archive in Kew.

Dated at Penrith on October 30th 1746, the dying speech of Robert Lyon describes the persecution of the Episcopal Church in Scotland, particularly by the Duke of Cumberland, and declares his detestation of both Roman Catholicism and Presbyterianism. He outlined his belief in 'passive obedience' and 'the divine right of Kings', and condemns the current monarchy as traitors. He declared that he joined 'the Prince's' [Charles Edward Stuart] cause to serve as their priest. Praising the conduct of the Jacobites, he described the destruction of St Ninians Church as accidental. Finally, he urged his countrymen to consider the cost of 'violating Gods Laws', and urges on them the fidelity and allegiance they owe their 'native and only rightful sovereign'.

The scale of the blast was extremely large. Whilst black powder is difficult to work out by quantity due to how finely it is ground, a barrel of eight Scots Gallons would be approximately 240 pounds of powder. If there were over 100 barrels as recorded in the church and we calculate on the basis of 100 barrels, this is around 24,000 pounds of black powder inside the church.

By way of comparison, Guy Fawkes had 5,500 lbs of gunpowder placed under the House of Lords for his assassination attempt of 1605, which has been modelled today as having significant structural damage.

So why not such a great deal more damage? An extrapolated plan shows that the equivalent impact on St Ninians of the 21st Century would be significant. Simply put, the population density and building density was vastly lower in 1746—flying debris can often account for additional damage and injuries. The other saving grace may have been the structure of the church itself. It would likely have had heavier walls of masonry construction, which may have helped direct the blast skywards.

In 1747 James Mackie, minister of the parish, petitioned the King reporting 'the rebels' use of his church as a store for gun powder, and its destruction when they fled the town; and on the resulting loss of revenue to the poor of his parish.' The king responded with £200, but the temporary church built across the road was to become the permanent church.

Over subsequent years the legend has been that the Jacobites blew up the church as they retreated—documented history often favours the victorious, of course. Regardless, the tower is a remarkable survivor of a magnificent church, and perhaps it is time that those who lost their lives are remembered more formally.

* * *

Dr David Mitchell is Director of Cultural Assets at Historic Environment Scotland and responsible for some of Scotland's most treasured places, collections and archives. He has lived in Stirling for 40 years and is Chair of the Smith Art Gallery

and Museum (Scotland's best wee museum!) and a Trustee of Stirling District Tourism. He is proud to be from Stirling, and loves to explore its rich history.

Baird and Hardie

David Kinnaird

Visitors to Stirling's Broad Street will be familiar with a weatherworn grey plaque mounted on the wall of Gideon Grey's 1760 extension to the old Tolbooth Jail. The plaque is of more recent vintage, unveiled on May Day 1966, and looking out on the Mercat Cross, the centrepiece of weekly markets in the bustling Royal Burgh for many centuries, and the location of whippings, brandings and all manner of public punishments—so that all could witness the consequence of crimes against the Commonwealth.

Its words are simple—and intriguing:

> IN MEMORY OF
> JOHN BAIRD AND ANDREW HARDIE
> WHO WERE PUBLICLY HANGED HERE
> ON 8th SEPTEMBER 1820
> ...FOR THE CAUSE OF JUSTICE AND TRUTH

Heroes, for sure, to be so honoured. But why? Many locals know little or nothing about these men—yet their plaque is a place of pilgrimage for many, every year, coming to Stirling from all over the world to see it. Even in Lockdown, in 2020, a small coterie of admirers gathered—safely distanced—to honour the anniversary of their passing.

To understand why these men are so revered, we need to look back to the first decades of the 19th Century.

Britain was in crisis. Unemployment was soaring, and many provincial labourers were left jobless as long-established communities were decimated by the Industrial Revolution. The Corn Laws, introduced that same year, protected the profits of merchants by stemming the flow of cheap imported grain—leaving much of the poverty-stricken population hungry. Scottish weavers found themselves at the forefront of a campaign for change – striking for nine weeks, in 1812, after employers had refused to pay a wage increase agreed upon by the High Court.

In April of 1820 posters appeared in Scotland's cities, urging the common people to support a national strike, calling for the repeal of the Corn Law and demanding that the common man be granted the right to vote—a privilege enjoyed at the time by only 2% of the male population.

One 'Radical Weaver', Andrew Hardie, joined the protest—leading some sixty men on a slow march to the Carron Iron Works, where the rebels hoped to find arms.

Struggling through driving wind and rain, his group was reduced to a weary and bedraggled twenty-five by the time it reached Condorrat, where they were joined by another Radical commander, John Baird.

Approaching Bonnymuir, the protesters came into conflict with soldiers. Lieutenant Edward Hodgson, of the 10th Hussars, the commanding officer of the troop, claimed that the Radicals were the aggressors, but others disputed his account. Shots were fired on both sides and many of the rebels—including Baird and Hardie—were captured.

Politics aside, the Lieutenant was impressed by John Baird's bearing. Imprisoned with the other rebels at Stirling Castle, the young Radical stepped forward and declared,

'Sir, if there is to be any severity exercised towards us, let it be on me. I am their leader, and have caused them being here. I hope that I alone may suffer.'

And suffer he would.

The authorities determined that an example should be made of the rebel leaders, in order to stifle what the *Stirling Journal* condemned as a *'shameful militancy'*.

A former soldier, serving in Argentina and Spain with the 2nd Battalion of the 95th Regiment of Foot—the Rifle Brigade—Baird had shown more concern for his men than for himself. His followers would face Transportation to the Australian Penal Colonies. As leaders of this insurrection, though, Baird and Hardie, were sentenced to be hanged for the crime of Sedition, and then beheaded—the statutory punishment for the offence of High Treason—both to be carried out at Stirling's Mercat Cross, on September 21st 1820.

Taken from Stirling Castle to the Tolbooth, the calmness with which the weavers sat in prayer in the hours before their execution unsettled the already anxious authorities. Every precaution possible was taken to temper the passions of the mob.

For every four inhabitants of the town, there would be one armed soldier present—so great was fear that the outraged population would descend into riot and rampage. The Glasgow Hangman, engaged to despatch the pair, had been secretly escorted into the town two days before. Fearful of his safety, he would remain hooded and anonymous until he departed the Burgh the following day.

As 2pm, the hour of their final reckoning, approached, they asked if they might bid their comrades—still imprisoned in the cells—a sad farewell. In the weeks that followed, these nineteen young men would be Transported to a lifetime of penal servitude in New South Wales.

One newspaper, The Courier, described how '...the executioner was then called in to pinion the prisoners. This they submitted to, almost cheerfully... declaring that they were now ready to proceed to the scaffold.'

The expected riot did not occur. No more blood was shed.

To 'the credit of the humanity of the inhabitants of this place, very few attended the execution', wrote a reporter from The Times of London, noting that 'the crowd seemed almost entirely composed of people from the country, this being the Market-Day'.

The Sheriff, Ranald MacDonald—Bonnymuir falling within the rural rubric of his authority—had demanded that the pair make no political speech from the scaffold—nothing that might inflame the passions of the mob—but agreed that they could speak upon Scripture.

Baird spoke to the tearful crowd from the gallows: '*I entreat you, notice your Bibles, and conduct yourself soberly; mind religion at all times; but be not regardless of Justice and Reason on every subject.*'

He then added, with rather more venom,

'*Although this day we die an ignominious death by unjust laws, our blood, which in a very few minutes will flow over this scaffold, will cry to Heaven for vengeance, and may it be the means of our afflicted Countrymen's speedy redemption.*'

The crowd cheered and seemed to surge forward. Nervous guardsmen started, raising their rifles, and a moment's panic swept through the street—but quickly passed.

Scolded by the Sheriff, Baird apologised for any anxiety his words might have caused, urging them to go quietly home and read their Bibles, once the execution was over. He then led the crowd in singing from the Fifth Psalm:

> Give ear unto my words, O Lord, my meditations weigh.
> Hear my loud cry, my King, my God; for I to thee will pray.
> Lord, thou shalt early hear my voice: I early will direct
> My pray'r to thee; and, looking up, an answer will expect.

...words which, in their way, were a far *more* militant call for Justice than his previous outburst.

Nooses were put about their necks. The pair shook hands and embraced – as far as their bonds would permit. After a moment Hardie drew a white cambric handkerchief from his pocket, a signal to their executioner that they were prepared for what was to come.

According to *The Courier*, '*they were immediately thrown off and died without a struggle*'. After hanging for half an hour, the pair were cut down, and preparations for the final requirement of the sentence for High Treason—beheading—began.

Angry cries and chants of '*Murder!*' met the black-hooded executioner as he raised his axe over Hardie's corpse, the neck draped loosely over the block by the Sheriff's Officers: '*after two powerful strokes, a third slight touch was still necessary to sever some of the adhering fibres and skin*'. He held the head aloft and cried '*This is the head of a traitor!*'.

Sickened, the crowd immediately dispersed.

Their decapitated bodies cleaned and dressed by a local goodwife, Granny Duncan, they were buried together in an unmarked plot outside the walls of Stirling Castle, where they remained for 27 years. On 20th July, 1847, their remains were exhumed and carried to Sighthill Cemetery, Glasgow... though one local tradition has it that this was a bluff, intended to thwart those who might seek to desecrate their resting place, and that their bones remain within the Burgh to this day.

Their Sighthill monument bears a verse, beginning:

> 'Shades of the slaughtered! shall the blood
> Spilt on the block be ever dim?
> Behold! the blushing crimson flood
> Hath called for vengeance unto Him!'

Echoes, perhaps, of Baird's beloved Fifth Psalm—though it's ironic that the memory of these two men endures not simply because of the savagery of their end, or the bloodshed which might have followed, had their killing resulted in the riot the magistrates so wrongly predicted… but because they, at the last, proved the power of human dignity, compassion and brotherhood.

* * *

David Kinnaird is an actor, writer, historian and folklore specialist with a lasting passion for the mysteries and histories of Stirling's oddest books and crannies—a familiar figure to locals and visitors in his regular guise as the Burgh's notorious 'Happy Hangman', Jock Rankin, and as Creative Director of the Old Town Jail. His abstruse musings can be heard on the popular Patreon podcast, 'Spooks and Bogles'.

Christian MacLagan: She'd Make a Jolly Good Fellow

Morag Cross

When you look at denim jeans, or naval uniforms, you don't think of large, heavy volumes about ancient Scotland. However, just as plants convert sunlight into flowers, money from producing blue dye in India, was converted into Scottish archaeology. Christian MacLagan (1811-1901) was a pioneering female scholar and archaeologist in Stirling, and since her death in 1901, many legends have grown up around her. Sometimes the first women to break through professional or legal barriers have to be very determined and strong minded, which is often labelled 'difficult'. We can call them 'doughty' or 'formidable', but would we like them if we met them today? Possibly not! It can be easier to admire some such ladies than to like them, and of course, everyone is a product of their own times, no matter how 'advanced' some of their views are.

Several of the stories about Christian come from her own words, but she was a complex personality, who sometimes said one thing, but did the opposite. So it's interesting to track the evidence for how accurate some of these legends are. Christian has generated a low-level mythology in the Stirling area as a local heroine of feminism and scientific approaches to ancient monuments. But she's undergone what can only be described as 'reputational inflation'! It's only as recently as 2003 that she was called *'allegedly Britain's first female archaeologist'*, but this tentative suggestion was repeated so often that it solidified into an 'established fact'. When Historic Environment Scotland announced her commemorative plaque in 2018, she was *'Scotland's first female archaeologist'*. A local history book from 2019 proposes her as *'arguably the first female archaeologist in the world'*, indeed a challenging claim!

Christian doesn't need to be 'the first' to be an extraordinary figure in her own right – we place too much importance on competitive ranking of achievements. Defining our earliest woman archaeologist is almost impossible—massive Internet use means that inevitably, even earlier pioneers are constantly emerging. Alicia Spottiswoode (known as 'Lady John Scott', 1810–1900), was Christian's exact contemporary. Spottiswoode undertook organised digs in Berwickshire in the early 1860s, and so pre-dates Christian. No matter how you define 'archaeologist' (using science, trying to test theories by observation) or 'antiquarian' (an older, less objective approach with folklore and wishful thinking!), there are earlier such women in England (Catherine Hutton, 1756–1846 or Frances Stackhouse Acton, 1794–1881), Ireland (Elizabeth Rawdon, Lady Moira, 1731–1808, and Elizabeth Stokes, 1832–1900) and more will undoubtedly appear.

So, which tales were based on Christian's own words, and was she exaggerating? She was a woman of very strong convictions, who nursed resentments when she felt she'd been treated unfairly. She was a highly intelligent, well-educated woman who expected her opinions about stone circles, hillforts and battles to

be taken seriously. Yet Christian was marooned in a time and society when women were legally unable to attend university or vote, and she was well aware of those disadvantages.

As Christian was entering previously 'masculine' areas of activity (recording hillforts, publishing books, dealing with architects), the men who met her probably had no idea how to treat her. They had never dreamed a woman would want to examine and survey prehistoric sites, and then publish her findings in academic journals. She knew the difference between traditional folklore, and proven facts, backed with real evidence. Unfortunately, some of Christian's main ideas were just wrong, as should have been obvious to her at the time. She thought that small, dark 'chambered tombs' were houses, although nobody lived in anything similar anywhere else in the world. She carefully gathered drawings, books and letters from noted scholars and built her case for stone circles being the ruins of circular houses.

It was said she measured the stone circles with her umbrella, instead of measuring tapes. This seems very unlikely—a good way to make fun of a serious female scholar was to pretend they couldn't perform technical, or 'male' tasks, like drawing an accurate plan. So we can disregard this, unless she had marked her umbrella handle with feet and inches for convenience. This would be ingenious, sensible even, but she'd still need some basic surveying tapes or knotted cords as well.

Another legend about Christian is her relationship with the nation's oldest and most prestigious historical association, the Society of Antiquaries of Scotland, based in Edinburgh. This institution had its own museum and library, and its annual journal was regarded as equal to an 'official', authoritative record. Although Queen Victoria was their patron, by 1870 they still had no female members. The Society didn't expect ladies to want to attend their evening meetings, behaving like an exclusive gentleman's club. For 90 years, this had never been an issue until a small number of well-read, financially independent women, began collecting, recording and donating more material to their museum from the 1860s onwards.

Christian belonged to an excellent general subscription library in Stirling, but the largest collection of Scottish history books, papers and drawings was that of the Society of Antiquaries in Edinburgh. She always 'went to the top', that is, to the best sources, and expected, naturally, to get access to this vast resource for her own research. Here, the story becomes complicated…

Christian published four books, and 15 papers between 1872 and 1898 (some articles appeared as brief summaries, a common practice at the time). She covered prehistoric stone circles, hillforts, Iron Age 'brochs' (round towers), early medieval tombstones on Iona, and Pictish and other carved stones. This is a prodigious output even by today's standards, when excavations can languish unpublished for decades!

Because only Society members (called 'Fellows') could attend the meetings in Edinburgh, and they were all men, Christian could not attend or read out her own paper. So the secretary, Dr John Stuart, presented it on her behalf, in exactly the same way as he stood in for all the men who wrote contributions but lived too far away to attend. Her first article, '*On the round castles and ancient dwellings of the valley of the Forth, and its tributary the Teith*' was heard on 12 December 1870. The Society was so impressed by her scholarship, that they wanted to show their respect. They had already created a new class of membership specifically for Lady John Scott earlier in 1870—details of Scott's excavations of prehistoric tombs and wooden walkways in Berwickshire, were presented (by men) at meetings in 1864 and 1868.

It took the Society only three weeks to appoint Christian as their second Lady Associate, at their very next meeting in January, 1871. This was not the action of an eminent body of men ignoring, or dismissing a frivolous, empty-headed old maid, but a mark of genuine appreciation. The Society already had men as 'Corresponding Associates' who didn't vote or hold office. Because the 'Lady Associates' were based on this existing male category, they also had the same very limited rights.

It's been claimed that Christian's work was only 'accepted' because it was '*transcribed by a man*'. However, this isn't correct—'transcribing' is 'making a copy of something', and Christian wrote all her own papers out, by hand! Nor did she ever use a pseudonym to hide her sex. Christian was a very common Victorian woman's name, although now it's considered masculine. Her paper was accepted immediately, and published under her own authorship. Christian was sufficiently proud of her status that, for ten years, she signed all her papers as 'Lady Associate', along with her first book, the fully illustrated *'Hill Forts and Stone Circles of Scotland'*, published in 1875.

We don't have space here to discuss her theories that, after farmers removed stones from ruined brochs, their foundations were 'mistakenly' identified as stone circles. Even in her lifetime this was thought to be a rather bizarre idea. But as an eyewitness observer, who described and recorded such sites, other scholars referred to Christian's factually-based plans and descriptions. Her somewhat eccentric interpretations are best examined elsewhere.

Christian, like her male contemporaries, needed to consult the latest archaeological research—but here she ran into problems. The Society of Antiquaries don't seem to have produced printed regulations that explicitly barred women from using their library (the public certainly visited their museum). However, she obviously experienced objections from an official, who is presently unidentified! On a study trip to Sardinia in 1881, she consulted anything in the *'library of the university in a manner which home authorities would not have accorded'*. Although I'm still researching this, Christian may have been been the victim of an unwritten, and unofficial, policy of frustrating her access. Whether she had actually fallen out with a staff member, or was just the 'wrong' sex, the anger and frustration she felt were genuine and long-lasting.

An obvious option was to try and use either the Advocates', or the Signet Libraries in Edinburgh, which were generally open to lawyers only. Outsiders required special permission, which was considered on a case by case basis. The all-male legal establishment generally held very traditional views about woman's roles, which definitely weren't among their legal tomes. A previous historian, Agnes Strickland, had tactfully enlisted the Signet librarian's help to borrow original documents (not allowed today!). Agnes implies that she carried out both her Signet and Advocates' archives research 'at a distance', possibly by post. Christian was far more 'hands-on', and really needed to feel involved. Such ladies' scholarship, and how they circumvented any unspoken rules, is only now being properly analysed.

One advantage of ambiguous regulations is that they can be applied inconsistently, as an investigation of the Advocates' Library records shows. At least as early as 1877, and possibly even before this, women were occasionally approved to consult or borrow the Advocates' books in person. Christian's name has not yet appeared in the Advocates' Library minutes so she presumably didn't apply. Nevertheless, this shows that there were other potential archives, which Christian chose not to use, instead focusing on the unattainable Antiquaries' collection. Once more, her grievances about library usage are only partially justified—the Advocates' curators were prepared to treat potential female readers seriously, had Christian only applied.

Christian was obviously willing to use the grand-sounding 'Lady Associate' title in her own work. But—as it didn't include a reader's ticket to her beloved history books, 'Associate' just sounded impressive. It conferred no practical benefits, except a free printed copy of the annual *'Proceedings'*.

As a book-lover, Christian naturally resented, and became increasingly outspoken about, her unfair exclusion from the Antiquaries' vast store of volumes in Edinburgh. It wasn't necessarily 'personal' against her, as an individual, but she was definitely a victim of the general 19th century assumption that all amateur historians would be male. She was forced to find alternative sources of information, and dedicated her 1881 book *'Chips from Old Stones'*, to an English vicar for his kindness in giving her *'the benefit of... his goodly library'*.

Her comments about Sardinia show how deeply her 'banishment' (never-stated, but effectual) from the Antiquaries' extensive archives had offended her. The Society apparently saw no need to even contemplate whether 'ladies' might wish to join their private clique. Nowadays we can easily recognise this as 'sexism', but that's a modern term unknown to the Victorians. She was certainly subject to sexual discrimination, as were all women, to varying degrees, but Christian was very aware of how ridiculous and pointless such customary, longstanding practices were.

Quite understandably, as a reaction to this segregation, Christian stopped contributing to the Society of Antiquaries. Instead she joined the recently founded Stirling Natural History and Archaeology Society in 1880. Here, her legend needs to be corrected with fact. We can either believe everything that Christian writes about how she was treated, or we can ask some additional questions, and see that she was a complicated, often self-contradictory character. For instance, she remarks sarcastically in 1894, *'Though [I am] a woman and therefore unworthy of being a member of any Antiquarian Society... we may add our feeble testimony on the... question'*. Here, she is being extremely disingenuous—that is, she complains about one thing, and yet does the complete opposite. In 'real life', by 1894, Christian had actually belonged to the respected Stirling Archaeological Society for 14 years. In 1879, the Stirling society recorded 93 male—and 36 female members: *'the attendance of members, both male and female, has been gratifying'*. In addition, she could easily have joined the equally-reputable Glasgow Archaeological Society (founded 1856), whose rules *'admit ladies also, it is hoped that... many... may be induced to take an interest'*. Women certainly attended Glasgow meetings from at least 1867, but presumably without Christian.

According to her obituary, Christian told the Antiquaries in Edinburgh, *'If I am not good enough to come in... as a member, I am too good to be left out in your Hall'*. But in the Smith Museum, Stirling, Christian could have stood at the front of the lecture theatre and personally delivered each of the eight papers she wrote for them. Instead, she sat in the audience, and listened to others read out her words, including another woman. Her personal secretary-assistant, Jessie Colvin, presented no fewer than four of them—so Christian could, and did, exaggerate to make her point more forcefully. She deliberately chose not to stand up and speak for herself, when she could have done so despite being female.

Another myth about Christian is that her family was rich. In fact, she was brought up by a single parent with a very limited income. Her father, an unsuccessful small-scale whisky distiller, died young and her mother raised four young children in small, rented flats in Edinburgh and Stirling. Here we return to the deep blue dye we started with. The MacLagans lived on an allowance sent back from Kolkata, India by her uncle, who traded in indigo. This was a valuable plant that produced the ubiquitous colouring for sailor's uniforms and modern denim clothing. Christian didn't inherit her own personal cash windfall (from her brother, another indigo planter) until she was nearly 50. Before that, she lived a very modest, restricted existence attending church and looking after her disabled mother.

She only started her impressive writing and publishing career when she was nearly 60, using her indigo-derived fortune to produce her impressive legacy of folklore, travelogue and commentary on 'the past as she saw it'. We may interpret our heritage differently, but she was a sincere, and serious, scholar, who began her comprehensive gazetteer, 'Hill Forts and Stone Circles', by stating her methods. She *'recorded the facts gathered [by] observations... made from personal examination of the remains described'*. She was trying to be exact, and precisely describe what she saw, and so we are only following her own practice if we look critically at her rich legacy of drawings and descriptions. Christian herself deserves the respect of accuracy. She had to act as a true ground-breaker, in a society that was biased against clever, articulate and self-confident women. Even if we try and cut out the 'legends' and stick to the facts, she remains a plentiful and engaging source of stories about Scotland's ancient landscapes.

* * *

Morag Cross is an independent researcher and archaeologist, specialising in histories of buildings and land ownership. Her archival research explores the unexpected links between previously unknown figures, especially women, their social networks and wider contexts. She has worked on over 80 projects, including Glasgow City Council's official World War I website, and compiling business histories for the Glasgow University's 'Mackintosh Architecture' website. Morag has also investigated Edinburgh's India Buildings, Victoria St, and both industrial and medieval archaeology, including the Dominican Friary, Goosecroft Road in Stirling, and other sites in Edinburgh and across Scotland. She's currently looking at some lesser-known early female historians and travellers.

Wallace and Cambuskenneth

Nick Brand

We all know the story of Wallace's betrayal by Monteith at Robroyston, and his subsequent removal to London to be executed for alleged treason in the most barbarous method possible.

He was sentenced to be hanged, drawn and quartered, a peculiarly English ritual which was supposed to ensure that the 'guilty' could not rise again on Judgement Day—vengeance even beyond the grave.

His head was spiked on London Bridge, and the four quarters of his mutilated body displayed in Newcastle, Berwick, Perth and Stirling, as a warning to all who transgressed against the rule of Longshanks. And there his story ended—with no final resting place for Scotland's best-known hero.

Or did it?

Wallace's maternal uncle was a member of the priesthood, at Dunipace by Stirling, whose original residence was at one time Kilspindie, in the Carse of Gowrie. It was due to his influence that Wallace was said to have been educated in Dundee, along with John Blair who became his chaplain and biographer, where according to Blind Harry his first skirmish with the English took place. It is a known fact that he and Andrew De Moray co-operated in the Battle of Stirling

Bridge on September 11th 1297, winning the battle against a much stronger English force, in the name of King John Balliol. What is also known is that Wallace's uncle had links with the monks of Cambuskenneth Abbey, which lies in the fold of the Forth a few hundred yards from the site of the battle itself.

Following Wallace's execution and dismemberment, one quarter of his mutilated body was displayed on the repaired and rebuilt Stirling Bridge. No doubt this was thought by the English overlords to be a fitting place to show off their grim trophy. And this is where the legend starts.

As previously stated, Wallace had links through his uncle to the monks at Cambuskenneth. At that time, the church was far more militant than nowadays, and many church leaders (and no doubt their subordinates) were fiercely loyal to Scotland and the cause of freedom. The legend states that a group of these monks issued from the Abbey one dark night and retrieved the remains of Wallace's body, with the intention of giving it a Christian burial inside the grounds of the Abbey itself, and this they did, telling no-one outside the Abbey of their actions, which would have brought fatal recriminations upon the Abbey. Longshanks was well known to be no respecter of the Scottish Church.

Cambuskenneth Abbey is, sadly, mostly ruined now, and apart from the main tower little remains bar foundations and low (ground level) walls. Local tradition however still marks the spot where it is said that Wallace's remains were interred by the loyal monks. Walk past the tower to your left, and then east along the inches-high wall, itself running almost due east. A little way along, just to your right (the south of the wall) is a small stone embedded in the ground, perpendicular to the remains of the wall. It's about 18 inches long and maybe six inches wide, orientated roughly north to south. At the southern end, faintly discernible although badly eroded, can still be made out the initials "WW" in antique script. A coincidence, you might think, or perhaps something placed later to give substance to the legend?

Stand at the southern end of the stone and look north along it. What do you see? The stone points straight towards the Abbey Craigs, the scene of Wallace's greatest triumph. The massive rock on which he and De Moray stood to direct the course of the battle with their horns and trumpeters…

So is it true? No-one knows, but it's a nice wee story. I personally would like to think that the good monks of Cambuskenneth did their Christian duty to the relative of a friend, and helped avert at least some of Longshanks' malevolence. It's worth a visit if you are in the vicinity. And funnily enough, you will often find on visiting that the stone has a small white rose placed on it. Some of us remember.

* * *

Nick Brand—mid-60s, and always interested in Scottish History, which eventually led to a BA (Hons) in History via the Open University in 2016, the final 2 years concentrating exclusively on Scottish history. A member of the Society of William Wallace for many years, and webmaster of the Society's website for the past five years or so, contributing several articles to the site as information is discovered—or previously uncovered. Still actively tracking down sources for the stories from Wallace's times.

Image Credits

Front Cover: Cover image showing detail from the National Wallace Monument is courtesy of Stirling District Tourism, and reproduced by kind permission of the copyright holder.

Frontispiece Artwork: The National Wallace Monument on Abbey Craig and the City of Stirling, shown courtesy of Stirling District Tourism, and reproduced by kind permission of the copyright holder.

Contents Page Artwork: Stirling Castle and the surrounding area. Image by Kamyq at Pixabay, and reproduced under the Pixabay licence.

Introduction Artwork: The Church of the Holy Rude and Valley Cemetery, Stirling. Image by Kamyq at Pixabay, and reproduced under the Pixabay licence.

The Wolves of Stirling: The wolf carving and inscription on Stirling Council's Wolfcraig building, Dumbarton Rd. (page iv). Image courtesy of Dr David Mitchell and reproduced by kind permission of the copyright holder.

John Cowane: Son of the Rock: The recently refurbished John Cowane statue above the entrance to Cowane's hospital, next to the Church of the Holyrude (page 4). Image courtesy of Dr David Mitchell and reproduced by kind permission of the copyright holder.

The Black Boy Fountain: The Black Boy Fountain in central Stirling's Allanpark (page 12). Image courtesy of The Stirling Smith Art Gallery and Museum and reproduced by kind permission of the copyright holder.

Legends and Lore of Logie Old Kirk: Old Logie Kirk in its tranquil setting at Blairlogie (page 21). Image courtesy of Dr David Mitchell and reproduced by kind permission of the copyright holder.

Legends of the Deep: Stirling as a Maritime Town: Stirling's bustling riverside in years gone by (page 26). Image courtesy of The Stirling Smith Art Gallery and Museum and reproduced by kind permission of the copyright holder.

The Beheading Stone of Mote Hill: The Beheading Stone, on Stirling's Mote Hill (page 39). Image courtesy of The Stirling Smith Art Gallery and Museum and reproduced by kind permission of the copyright holder.

The Staffman: The executioner's cloak, on exhibition in the Stirling Smith Art Gallery and Museum (page 44). Image courtesy of The Stirling Smith Art Gallery and Museum and reproduced by kind permission of the copyright holder.

The First Earl of Stirling: Argyll's Lodging, the tower house that belonged to the Earl of Stirling and was extended by the 9th Earl of Argyll when he took on the house in the late 17th century (page 53). Image courtesy of Dr Thomas Christie and reproduced by kind permission of the copyright holder.

John Damian: The Bird Man of Stirling Castle: Stirling Castle, pictured on Castle Hill. Quite a drop for John Damian and his wings (page 59)! Image by DerWeg at Pixabay, and reproduced under the Pixabay licence.

The Barnwell Brothers: The Barnwell brothers memorial in Causewayhead, Stirling (page 64). Image courtesy of Dr David Mitchell and reproduced by kind permission of the copyright holder.

St Ninians: The Day the Village Exploded: Details of the fateful day St Ninians exploded, depicted on a fan within the Stirling Smith Art Gallery and Museum's collection (page 75). Image courtesy of The Stirling Smith Art Gallery and Museum and reproduced by kind permission of the copyright holder.

Baird and Hardie: The Tolbooth and Mercat Cross in Stirling's Broad Street (page 82). The Tolbooth from the Church of the Holy Rude on Stirling's Castle Wynd (page 87). Images courtesy of Dr David Mitchell and reproduced by kind permission of the copyright holder.

Christian MacLagan: She'd Make a Jolly Good Fellow: Stirling's Wood Carvings Trail includes a Celtic cross for Christian beside the Stirling Smith Art Gallery and Museum, by artist Tommy Craggs. Her archaeologist's trowel and paper for wax rubbings are shown (page 93). The only word on Christian's tombstone is her first name in the Greek alphabet. She lies beside her mother in the Old Town Cemetery, Stirling (page 98). Images courtesy of Morag Cross and reproduced by kind permission of the copyright holder.

Wallace and Cambuskenneth: The remaining tower of Cambuskenneth Abbey (page 104). Image courtesy of Dr David Mitchell and reproduced by kind permission of the copyright holder.

About Stirling District Tourism: Image showing detail from the National Wallace Monument and the surrounding area (page 112) is shown courtesy of Stirling District Tourism, and reproduced by kind permission of the copyright holder.

About Stirling District Tourism

An independent local charity, Stirling District Tourism manages *Legends at the Monument*, providing a welcoming experience for visitors and local residents at our coffee house and gift shop.

The charity uses all funds raised to support educational and heritage activities in the greater Stirling area, and is proud to have provided visitor services at Legends for over 25 years - aiming to make a visit to Stirling and the National Wallace Monument a truly world class experience.

For details of new and forthcoming books from Extremis Publishing, including our monthly podcasts, please visit our official website at:

www.extremispublishing.com

or follow us on social media at:

www.facebook.com/extremispublishing

www.linkedin.com/company/extremis-publishing-ltd-/

www.ingramcontent.com/pod-product-compliance
Lightning Source LLC
Chambersburg PA
CBHW081620100526
44590CB00021B/3525